Heroes and Villains

ADOLF HITLER

Other books in the Heroes and Villains series include:

King Arthur
Al Capone
Frederick Douglass
Oskar Schindler

Heroes and Villains

ADOLF HITLER

Don Nardo

LUCENT
BOOKS ®

THOMSON
™
GALE

San Diego • Detroit • New York • San Francisco • Cleveland • New Haven. Conn. • Waterville. Maine • London • Munich

THOMSON

™

GALE

For more information, contact
Lucent Books
27500 Drake Rd.
Farmington Hills, MI 48331-3535
Or you can visit our Internet site at http://www.gale.com

LIBRARY OF CONGRESS CATALOGING-IN-PUBLICATION DATA

Nardo, Don, 1947–
    Adolf Hitler / by Don Nardo.
        p. cm. — (Heroes and villains series)
Summary: A biography of the struggling Austrian artist who rose from obscurity
to power as the leader of the Nazi party and, later, the German nation and whose
ambitions led the world to war.
Includes bibliographical references and index.
    ISBN 1-56006-951-1 (hardback : alk. paper)
    1. Hitler, Adolf, 1889–1945—Juvenile literature. 2. Heads of state—Germany—
Biography—Juvenile literature. [1. Hitler, Adolf, Germany—History—1933–1945.] I.
Title. II. Series.
    DD247.H5 N35 2003
    943.086'092—dc21
                                                            2002003812

Printed in the United States of America

Contents

FOREWORD   6

INTRODUCTION
Memory of a False Messiah   8

CHAPTER 1
1889–1919: The Wellsprings of Hate   12

CHAPTER 2
1919–1923: Rise of a Demagogue   24

CHAPTER 3
1923–1933: Triumph of the Will   36

CHAPTER 4
1933–1939: A Nation Transformed   50

CHAPTER 5
1939–1942: The Third Reich at Its Zenith   64

CHAPTER 6
1943–1945: Death of a Twisted Dream   78

EPILOGUE
Monument to a Monster   91

Notes   96
For Further Reading   99
Major Works Consulted   100
Additional Works Consulted   103
Index   106
Picture Credits   111
About the Author   112

Good and evil are an ever-present feature of human history. Their presence is reflected through the ages in tales of great heroism and extraordinary villainy. Such tales provide insight into human nature, whether they involve two people or two thousand, for the essence of heroism and villainy is found in deeds rather than in numbers. It is the deeds that pique our interest and lead us to wonder what prompts a man or woman to perform such acts.

Samuel Johnson, the eminent eighteenth-century English writer, once wrote, "The two great movers of the human mind are the desire for good, and fear of evil." The pairing of desire and fear, possibly two of the strongest human emotions, helps explain the intense fascination people have with all things good and evil—and by extension, heroic and villainous.

People are attracted to the person who reaches into a raging river to pull a child from what could have been a watery grave for both, and to the person who risks his or her own life to shepherd hundreds of desperate black slaves to safety on the Underground Railroad. We wonder what qualities these heroes possess that enable them to act against self-interest, and even their own survival. We also wonder if, under similar circumstances, we would behave as they do.

Evil, on the other hand, horrifies as well as intrigues us. Few people can look upon the drifter who mutilates and kills a neighbor or the dictator who presides over the torture and murder of thousands of his own citizens without feeling a sense of revulsion. And yet, as Joseph Conrad writes, we experience "the fascination of the abomination." How else to explain the overwhelming success of a book such as Truman Capote's *In Cold Blood,* which examines in horrifying detail a vicious and senseless murder that took place in the American heartland in the 1960s? The popularity of murder mysteries and Court TV are also evidence of the human fascination with villainy.

Most people recoil in the face of such evil. Yet most feel a deep-seated curiosity about the kind of person who could commit a terrible act. It is perhaps a reflection of our innermost fears that we wonder whether we could resist or stand up to such behavior in our presence or even if we ourselves possess the capacity to commit such terrible crimes.

The Lucent Books Heroes and Villains series capitalizes on our fascination with the perpetrators of both good and evil by introducing readers to some of history's most revered heroes and hated villains. These include heroes such as Frederick Douglass, who knew firsthand the humiliation of slavery and, at great risk to himself, publicly fought to abolish the institution of slavery in America. It also includes villains such as Adolf Hitler, who is remembered both for the devastation of Europe and for the murder of 6 million Jews and thousands of Gypsies, Slavs, and others whom Hitler deemed unworthy of life.

Each book in the Heroes and Villains series examines the life story of a hero or villain from history. Generous use of primary and secondary source quotations gives readers eyewitness views of the life and times of each individual as well as enlivens the narrative. Notes and annotated bibliographies provide stepping-stones to further research.

Memory of a False Messiah

On a September day in 1934, the German town of Nuremberg was thrilled at the arrival of Adolf Hitler, leader of the Nazi Party, who had come to power as Germany's chancellor in January of the preceding year. William L. Shirer, an American journalist, witnessed what seemed to him an extraordinary spectacle that day in Nuremberg. Hitler swept into the town, he recalled, flanked by a phalanx of guards wearing armbands bearing the crooked arms of the swastika, the Nazi symbol. Thousands of other swastikas screamed from giant Nazi flags unfurled along the sides of houses and shops. As the motorcade advanced, waves of excited local citizens lined the narrow streets hoping to catch a glimpse of their idol, a short, tidy-looking, grim-faced individual. Later that night, Shirer wrote:

I got caught in a mob of ten thousand hysterics who jammed the moat in front of Hitler's hotel shouting: "We want our Führer [great leader]!" I was a little shocked at the faces, especially those of the women. . . . They looked up at him as if he were a Messiah [savior], their faces transformed.[1]

With the same blind adulation displayed at Nuremberg, people all across Germany accepted their new leader's grandiose promises of raising them to new heights of prestige and power. Theirs was the master race, he said; and it was his mission to see that "inferior" races and peoples did not get in the way of Germany's rightful destiny.

Yet in the fullness of time, the fruits of greatness the führer had promised the Germans turned to bitter ashes. A mere eleven years after that night in Nuremberg, the false Messiah was dead, Germany lay in ruins, and more than 40 million people had died in the most devastating conflict of all times. Hitler himself had instigated and launched the war; and in his capacity as a ruthless dictator, he had prosecuted it with unprecedented hatred, brutality, cruelty, and utter disregard for human life. "Never in history has such ruination—physical and moral—been associated with the name of one man," remarks historian Ian Kernshaw.

Hitler's name justifiably stands for all time as that of the chief instigator of the most profound collapse of civilization in modern

Thousands of German troops crowd in front of the podium, waiting for their idol, Adolf Hitler, to speak in the massive Nazi rally staged in Nuremberg in September 1934.

times. The extreme personal rule which an ill-educated beerhall demagogue [leader who manipulates the truth to gain power], racist bigot, [and] . . . self-styled national savior was allowed to acquire and exercise in a modern, economically advanced, and cultured land . . . was absolutely decisive in the terrible unfolding of events in those fateful . . . years.[2]

The Personification of Evil

Considering Hitler's enormous abuses of power and the terrible consequences of his misrule, succeeding generations have expressed amazement that such a destructive character could hold sway over the hearts and minds of millions. As Williams College scholar Robert G.L. Waite puts it:

Hitler's personality will continue to challenge those who seek to answer one of the most intriguing questions of all history: how it was possible for this strange little man, at once so banal [ordinary] and so terrible, to hold a great nation enthralled in cruel yet popular tyranny and to conquer a continent.[3]

The question of what made Hitler tick is difficult to answer with any certainty, partly because he was an enigma, a mysterious individual who con-

cealed many of his inner thoughts from those close to him. "You will never learn what I am thinking," he once told one of his generals. "And those who boast most loudly that they know my thoughts, to such people I lie even more."[4] So Hitler revealed one part of his personality to some people and other parts to others. To some he was reserved, even gentle and considerate; others saw his vicious, heartless, cold, and cruel side. In the memoirs of those who knew him are accounts of a reasonable man; others that speak about his charm; and still others that describe the violent tantrums of a crazed, twisted child in an adult's body. In the face of a veritable barrage of conflicting testimony, it was and remains hard to understand the man.

Because of the difficulty in analyzing Hitler from a subjective point of view, most historians and other interested observers have chosen to do so from an objective viewpoint, one based on his actions. These actions speak for themselves. First, he manipulated the German masses and the country's political system to seize absolute power; then he imposed a brutal dictatorship and built a gigantic and lethal war machine; he used this machine to invade Poland, France, Russia, and seize control of most of Europe; he oversaw the systematic mass murder of millions of Jews, Poles, Gypsies, and others; and he caused the needless deaths of millions of Germans by his poor strategy and fanatical insistence on continuing to fight even after the country's defeat was inevitable. For these infamous deeds, Adolf Hitler has come to be seen, with almost universal affirmation, as the personification of evil. Indeed, he has more than earned his reputation as perhaps the most infamous villain in history.

The Nazis as Heavies

Because they loyally protected him and carried out his brutal orders, Hitler's Nazi officers and storm troopers have come to be demonized as well. Abundant eyewitness testimony and documentary evidence attest to their horrible crimes against humanity. So it is hardly surprising that both they and their nefarious boss have long been recurring and highly serviceable "bad guys" in popular fiction. In today's modern, politically correct society, one must take care not to portray any of a wide range of individuals and groups in a negative light for fear of offending them; yet no one hesitates for a moment to cast Hitler and his Nazis as the heavies in novels, movies, television shows, cartoons, and video games. Moreover, audiences invariably cheer

on the hero who outwits, kills, or otherwise overcomes the Nazis, once more demonstrating the triumph of good over evil. (In reenactments of World War II, such heroes have been played by actors Humphrey Bogart, Errol Flynn, John Wayne, and Clint Eastwood to name only a few; more imaginative Nazi-fighters have included Indiana Jones, Captain Kirk, Tarzan, and Donald Duck.)

Thus, it has become perfectly acceptable, as well as entertaining, to invoke and ridicule the image of Hitler and his Nazi thugs. But there is a potential danger in portraying these men as mere cardboard villains; namely, we risk distancing ourselves from the true horror of their deeds. The naked fact is that Hitler was a real person who willfully caused misery, death, and destruction on a scale humanity had never before seen and has not seen since. He and his horrendous acts must never be forgotten, else the world runs the risk of allowing more such villains to repeat them. The most effective way to keep fresh the memory of what Hitler did is to examine his life and misdeeds in some detail. And that is the purpose of this volume.

Chapter One

1889–1919: THE WELLSPRINGS OF HATE

At the height of his power as Germany's dictator, in the late 1930s and early 1940s, Adolf Hitler wielded more direct personal power than any national leader in history. His every whim or wish carried the force of law, and by his orders millions of people were murdered, tortured, attacked, or harassed. As Robert Waite points out, he also

> set the standards for art, music, medicine, and poetry. . . . He dictated statutes which set forth the religion of household servants, the colors artists could use in paintings, the way lobsters were to be cooked in restaurants, and how physics would be taught in the universities. He decided whom Germans might marry, what they

could name their children, where they could be buried.[5]

Perhaps the most amazing thing about this man who held the fate of millions in his hands is how truly unimpressive he was from a personal standpoint. His physical and mental attributes, as well as his personal habits, were hardly what one might expect of a national idol worshiped by the masses. As an adult Hitler was about five feet eight and weighed roughly 150 pounds. His posture was poor, his chest somewhat sunken, his skin abnormally pale, his legs unusually short, his feet strangely large, his nose too big for his face (prompting him to grow his signature bushy mustache to help offset it), and his teeth brownish yellow and riddled with fillings. He also tended to drag his left foot when he walked. His only striking physical feature was his eyes, which many who knew him described as penetrating and compelling.

Hitler was no intellectual giant, either, though he clearly saw himself that way. To his credit he had a phenomenal memory for individual facts about a wide range of subjects, which he often rattled off to his associates, duly impressing them. One of his secretaries later recalled, "I often asked myself how one human brain could preserve so many facts."[6] Yet abundant evidence shows that Hitler's mind was undisciplined and that he lacked the interest or ability, or both, to deal with complex or difficult intellectual concepts. He tended instead to simplify ideas, often distorting their meaning, and to reduce them to slogans, sound bites, and other manageable units of data that suited his purposes. His great command of such facts often gave the impression that he was well-read in serious works of history, philosophy, and science; but in reality, almost all of his reading consisted of newspapers, pamphlets, and magazines.

Thus, in and of themselves, Hitler's natural gifts were insufficient to explain his popularity and rise to absolute power. Rather, his success seems to have stemmed from the attitudes and beliefs he acquired as a child and young man, and the consistent, untiring, and highly persuasive way he

He Spoke with His Eyes

Many people who met Hitler recalled his eyes and his penetrating gaze. One was a boyhood acquaintance, August Kubizek, who wrote in his 1955 memoir, The Young Hitler I Knew:

The eyes were so outstanding that one didn't notice anything else. Never in my life have I seen any other person whose appearance . . . was so completely dominated by the eyes. They were the light eyes of his mother but her somewhat staring, penetrating gaze was even more marked in the son and had even more force and expressiveness. It was uncanny how those eyes could change their expression, especially when Adolf was speaking. . . . In fact, Adolf spoke with his eyes, and even when his lips were silent one knew what he wanted to say. . . . If I am asked where one could perceive, in his youth, this man's exceptional qualities, I can only answer, "In the eyes."

expounded these ideas. Add to this the peculiar historical events and political and economic conditions in Germany during Hitler's youth; these made the country ripe for the rise of a leader who knew how to tell the people what they wanted to hear. The roots of his villainy, therefore, must be sought in the events and atmosphere of his youth, which both shaped his dangerous views and laid the fertile soil in which they would grow and spread.

An Unremarkable Home Life

Hitler's birth occurred on April 20, 1889 in the small Austrian town of Braunau am Inn. His father, Alois, was a lower–middle-class customs official. As a child, Alois bore his mother's last name—Shicklgruber—but later changed it to that of his stepfather, Johann Hitler (originally Hiedler) to cover up the fact that Alois was illegitimate. One of Alois's supervisors described him as "very strict, exacting, and pedantic [formal and precise], a most unapproachable person."[7] The elder Hitler treated young Adolf coldly and sternly, as he did Adolf's half-brother, Alois Jr., the product of a previous marriage. Both boys received whippings and perhaps suffered other abuses, so much so that Adolf expressed genuine relief when his father died in January 1903 at age sixty-six.

By contrast, young Adolf's mother, Klara Hitler, lavished love and attention on him. She probably tried to make up for her husband's cruelty by spoiling the boy, which angered her stepson, whom she apparently neglected. The grown-up and resentful Alois Jr. recalled:

"My stepmother always took his [Adolf's] part. He would get the craziest notions and get away with it. If he didn't have his way he got very angry. . . . He had no friends, took to no one and could be very heartless. He could fly into a rage over any triviality."[8]

Adolf's special relationship with his mother came to an untimely end after she was suddenly diagnosed with breast cancer in January 1907. Doctors performed a double mastectomy but to no avail; she died in December, leaving her son completely distraught. The family's Jewish doctor, Edward Bloch, later remembered: "In all my career, I never saw anyone so prostrate with grief as Adolf Hitler."[9]

Hitler later showed an extreme aversion to talking about his family and upbringing. In 1930, when some reporters attempted to find out about his youth, he told an aide, "These people must never find out who I am. They mustn't know where I come from or my family background."[10] This may well have been his way of covering up for those aspects of his early life he found embarrassing: his father's violent nature; a banal, unremarkable home life; his own childish emotional outbursts; a Jewish family doctor; and the

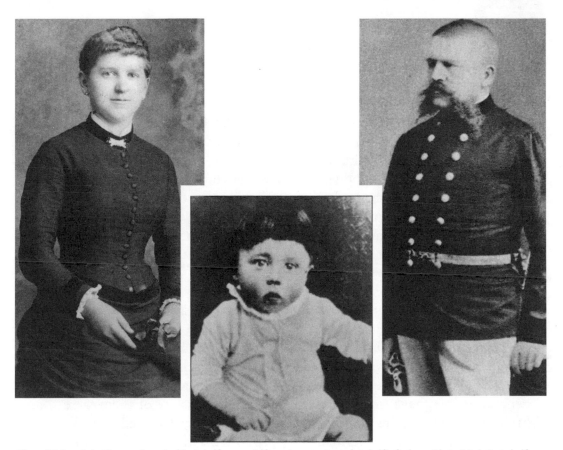

Klara Hitler, Adolf's mother (left); Adolf as an infant (center); and Adolf's father, Alois (right). Adolf later remembered his mother fondly and his father with contempt.

real possibility that Adolf had a Jewish grandfather. (Evidence shows that his grandmother, Alois's mother, worked as a maid in the home of a Jewish man named Frankenberger; the latter helped support Alois until he was fourteen, perhaps because Frankenberger's son was the boy's father.)

Inspired by Germany's Past

However the "dark secrets" Hitler perceived in his personal background may have affected him, they had less influence on the formation of his worldview than the larger cultural and political currents that swirled around him. First and foremost, there was the question of his "Germanness." Like many of his countrymen, as a teenager he came to identify strongly with Austria's German roots. In medieval and early modern times, Austria and other German regions had been united under the noble House of Habsburg as the Holy

Roman Empire, one of the strongest states in Europe. In 1871 the powerful German region of Prussia established a new German union that excluded Austria; however, World War I witnessed the emergence of a German-Austrian alliance. When this alliance was defeated by France, Britain, and the United States in 1918, the victors, known as the Allies, forbade Austria from reuniting with Germany, which angered many Germans and Austrians, including Hitler. "Today it seems providential that Fate should have chosen Braunau am Inn as my birthplace," he wrote in 1923, at age thirty-four.

> For this little town lies on the boundary between two German states which we of the younger generation . . . have made it our life's work to reunite by every means at our disposal. German-Austria must return to the great German mother country. . . . One blood demands one Reich. . . . Their sword will become our plow, and from the tears of war the daily bread of future generations will grow. And so this little city on the border seems to me the symbol of a great mission.[11]

Fascinated and inspired by the glories of Germany's past, Hitler liked reading about mythical German heroes. Especially appealing to him were the tall, blond Teutonic knights and gods of old, the so-called "Aryans," characters portrayed with dramatic flair in the operas of nineteenth-century German composer Richard Wagner (VOG-ner). (Wagner's many claims that Jews were freaks with tainted blood and his allusions to "the utterly alien element of the Jews"[12] had a profound effect on Hitler's own developing anti-Semitism.) Short, with dark hair, Hitler realized that he did not look like the ideal Aryan. Yet he fancied himself a member of that mythical superior race.

In school Hitler was not a good student. He was argumentative and placed most of the blame for his poor grades on his teachers, an excuse he clung to throughout his life. "When I recall my teachers at school," he stated in 1942, "I realize that half of them were abnormal. . . . The majority of them were somewhat mentally deranged."[13] This tendency to shift the blame became one of Hitler's hallmarks. Just as it was supposedly his teachers' fault that he did poorly in school, he later held that Germany's troubles in the years before he took power were not the fault of Germans, but of "enemies" in their midst, particularly Jews and Communists.

Aspects of a Twisted Psyche

Hitler was so unhappy at school that when he was sixteen he dropped out and for three years roamed about aimlessly, occasionally trying his hand at painting. Finally deciding he needed formal art training, in 1908, at age

Young Adolf Hitler (top row, center) in an elementary-school photo. He disliked most of his teachers and blamed them for his own shortcomings.

nineteen, he journeyed to Austria's capital, Vienna, in hopes of enrolling in that city's prestigious Arts Academy. Because of the poor quality of his sketches, however, the school rejected his application. In the four years that followed, he barely made a living working as a laborer and painting cheap postcards.

During these years of indecisiveness and drifting, many of the odd, often ominous personality traits that contributed to the whole of Hitler's twisted psyche were developing or had already developed. For enjoyment, for example, he was drawn to activities that embarrassed or hurt others, such as poking fun at amputees and deaf people. "He liked laughing," Nazi architect Albert Speer later recalled, "but it was always laughter at the expense of others."[14] In contrast, when displeased or unhappy, he either walked away and sulked or threw a tantrum. Hundreds of recollections of such tantrums by those who knew him have

17

survived. A Swedish visitor to Berlin remembered one outburst in which Hitler

> stopped in the middle of the room and stared straight ahead. His speech became more and more garbled, his whole behavior gave the impression of a person who was not at all himself. Sentences tumbled after one another.... [As he ranted and raved] his voice became increasingly indistinct and gradually one could no longer understand him. . . . At this moment he acted more like a demon in bad fiction than a human being. I looked at him in amazement.[15]

Hitler was as rigid as he was temperamental. He often stated his view that flexibility was a weakness and stubbornness a strength, and he was overtly embarrassed by the thought of changing his mind about anything. A boyhood acquaintance, August Kubizek, remembered "the unparalleled constancy in everything that he said and did. There was in his nature something firm, inflexible, immovable . . . rigid. Adolf simply could not change his mind or nature."[16] This rigidity extended to Hitler's personal habits, which were monotonously routine. He washed his hands many times each day; wore the same clothes and listened to the same records over and over until they

wore out; discussed the same subjects repeatedly, with almost no variation; and liked to see how fast he could dress and undress himself, timing himself or asking others to time him. In today's terminology, his personality was decidedly obsessive-compulsive.

Another and more frightening compulsive aspect of Hitler's psyche was a deep infatuation with death. He was fascinated by paintings depicting death and later, as Germany's dictator, enjoyed watching films of executions he had ordered. From an early age, he hated the moon because he viewed it as a dead thing, remarking to an associate: "In the moon a part of the terror still lives which the moon once sent down over the earth."[17] Hitler also considered eating meat to be the same thing as devouring a corpse and accordingly ridiculed meat-eaters. In addition, he regularly expressed the morbid fear that death was fast closing in on him, that he might never have the time to fulfill his grandiose ambitions.

An Intense Hatred for Jews
Still another side of the poor and homeless young Hitler's developing personality was a voracious capacity for blind, all-consuming hatred. In the years immediately preceding World War I, he spent much of his time reading articles about German history and various kinds of anti-Jewish literature. Thanks to constant exposure to the lat-

Obsessed with Wolves

As noted in this excerpt from Robert Waite's riveting book The Psychopathic God, *one of Adolf Hitler's numerous odd obsessions was a fascination for wolves.*

As a boy he was well pleased with his first name, noting that it came from the old German "Athalwolf"—a compound of Athal ("noble") and Wolfa ("wolf"). And "noble wolf" he sought to remain. At the start of his political career he chose "Herr Wolf" as his pseudonym. . . . One of [his dog] Blondi's pups, born towards the end of the war, he called "Wolf" and would allow no one else to touch or feed it. He named his headquarters in France *Wolfsschlucht* (Wolf's Gulch). In the Ukraine his headquarters were *Werwolf* (Man Wolf) and in East Prussia *Wolfsschanze* (Wolf's Lair). As he explained to a servant, "I am the Wolf and this is my den." He called his SS "My pack of wolves." . . . When he telephoned Winifred Wagner [the great composer's daughter-in-law], he would say "Conductor Wolf calling!" The secretary he kept longer than any other . . . was Johanna Wolf. She recalled that . . . [he] called her "Wölfin" (She-Wolf). One of his favorite tunes came from a Walt Disney movie. Often and absent-mindedly he whistled "Who's Afraid of the Big Bad Wolf?"

ter, including poisonous tracts by Wagner, he steadily developed an irrational fear of and intense hatred for Jews, which would later lead to some of his most evil acts. In the following excerpt from his earliest known anti-Semitic writing, which characterizes Jews in racial rather than religious terms, Hitler states:

Through a thousand years of inbreeding, often practiced within a very narrow circle, the Jew has in general preserved his race . . . much more rigorously than many of the peoples among whom he lives. And as a result, there is living amongst us a non-German, foreign race, unwilling and unable to sacrifice its racial characteristics. . . . [The Jew's] weapon is that public opinion which is never given utterance by the press, but is always led by it and falsified by it. . . . Everything which makes men strive for higher things, whether religion, socialism, or democracy, is for him only a means to an end, to the satisfaction of a lust for money and domination. His activities produce a racial tuberculosis among nations.[18]

This bizarre idea, that German Jews were not Germans but instead a separate and inferior race living inside Germany, was a product of Hitler's own ignorance and blind hatred. Jews had made up a small but important and productive minority of Germany's population for many centuries and were no less German than the nation's non-Jewish inhabitants. Ironically, Hitler had experienced many kindnesses from Jews; besides Dr. Bloch, who had lovingly seen Frau Hitler through her fatal illness, many of the shelters and soup kitchens that Adolf Hitler availed himself of in his homeless days were founded and supported by a German Jew. And the young homeless man received his only warm coat from a Jewish clothes merchant who took pity on him.

Unhappy in Vienna, in 1912 Hitler moved to Munich, in southern Germany. There he continued to drift about, working as a carpenter and poster painter until the outbreak of World War I in 1914, at which time he enlisted in the German army infantry. In

This photograph taken in World War I shows Hitler (at far left, bottom) posing with members of his platoon. Even then he blamed the Jews for Germany's troubles.

Hitler's Attempts to Impress Women

For various reasons, many women were attracted to Hitler and he enjoyed their attention. But he was also insecure about how he appeared to them and tried hard to project an image of strength and virility. One young woman, Pauline Kohler, later recalled (in a document collected in Walter Langer's Hitler Source Book) *how he tried to impress her by adopting the Nazi salute and ineptly bragging:*

I can hold my arm like that for two solid hours. I never feel tired when my storm troopers and soldiers march past me and I stand at this salute. I never move. My arm is like granite—rigid and unbending. But [Nazi leader Hermann] Goering can't stand it. He has to drop his hand after half an hour of this salute. He's flabby. But I am hard. For two hours I can keep my arm stretched out in the salute. That is four times as long as Goering. That means I'm four times stronger than Goering. It's an amazing feat. I marvel at my own power.

his four years in the military, he served as a message carrier and fought on the western front against the British. Temporarily blinded by poison gas during a battle, he was hospitalized for shell shock and fatigue and eventually received two medals for bravery. A comrade later described how Hitler, a loner who never asked for or went on leave, would often sit "in the corner of our mess [platoon] holding his head between his hands, in deep contemplation." Without warning, he would "leap up and, running about excitedly, say that in spite of our big guns victory would be denied us," because Germany's "invisible foes" posed a greater danger than the enemy.[19] Then he would launch into a tirade about these foes, namely, the "degenerate" Jews and Communists.

The Infamous "Stab in the Back"

Hitler's worst fears were realized when Germany lost the war, and not surprisingly he was extremely bitter, a feeling he shared with most Germans. Humiliated, early in 1919 they were forced to sign the Treaty of Versailles, which officially brought the conflict to a close and imposed very harsh penalties on Germany. The country had to cede some of its best industrial territories to the victors, pay huge reparations (moneys to compensate for the damages suffered by its opponents), and overall lost much power and prestige.

The traumatic effect the loss of the war had on the German people cannot be overstressed. As historian Crane Brinton explains:

> For the overwhelming majority of the German people, defeat in 1918 came as a great shock. The military authorities who ran the German Empire during the last years of the war had failed to report to the public German reverses on the battlefield. No fighting had ever taken place on German soil, and the Germans had got used to thinking of their armies as in firm possession of the foreign territories they had overrun. . . . Schooled in reverence for their military forces, the Germans could not grasp the fact that their armies had lost the war.[20]

Moreover, the harsh fact that German leaders had ordered their forces to surrender because they were no longer in any shape to fight was never effectively publicized in Germany. So the legend quickly grew that civilians at home—principally liberal politicians, Communists, and Jews—

In this rarely seen photograph taken on December 2, 1918, leaders from Britain, France, Italy, Greece, and other Allied countries draw up the Treaty of Versailles.

had somehow betrayed the nation. This so-called "stab in the back" soon became an article of faith among Germans of all walks of life, and it is therefore not surprising that so many of them later agreed with Hitler's denunciations of those who had supposedly sold the country out. "The German people wanted simple answers to their questions and simple solutions to their problems," wrote the late Princeton University scholar Erich Kahler.

Hitler gave them what they wanted. . . . He told his audiences that the Jews, the socialists, the bankers, and the Allies were responsible for Germany's woes. . . . He told the people what they wanted to hear, and he told it to them with remarkable effect.[21]

Therefore, the German people emerged from their defeat in World War I infected by large amounts of misinformation, misconceptions, ignorance, fear, and outright lies. By itself, perhaps, any one of these insidious negative factors would not have been enough to send Germany down a destructive path. But in combination with and manipulated by a twisted little man named Adolf Hitler, they would prove to be the wellsprings of the hate, arrogance, and brutality that would eventually lead the country toward oblivion.

Chapter Two

1919–1923: Rise of a Demagogue

Though the "stab in the back" Germany had supposedly suffered at the hands of traitors at home was only imaginary, many Germans firmly accepted it as real. Certainly, nearly all Germans felt humiliated by the Treaty of Versailles, which the Allies had forced on a defeated Germany. And young Adolf Hitler undoubtedly felt more humiliated, betrayed, and angry than the average person. He was greatly moved and proud when he heard about the bitter words spoken by Count Brockdorff-Rantzau, who represented Germany during the treaty's formal acceptance ceremony. "We are under no illusions," the count had said to the Allied leaders,

> as to the extent of our defeat and the degree of our powerlessness.

We know that the strength of the German arms is broken. We know the intensity of the hatred which meets us, and we have heard the victor's passionate demands that as the vanquished we shall be made to pay, and as the guilty we shall be punished. The demand is made that we shall acknowledge that we alone are guilty for having caused the war. Such confession in my mouth would be a lie.[22]

To a large extent, it was this sense of loss, betrayal, and humiliation that Hitler used to his own advantage when he began his political activities in the early 1920s. As a public speaker, he deftly manipulated his audiences, stroking their bruised German egos and playing on their fears of domination by the Allies. He did not hesitate to exaggerate or distort the facts and sometimes even to lie. By definition, his employment of false claims and promises in his speeches made him a demagogue; and demagogues were a dime a dozen in Germany at the time. But Hitler developed a remarkable skill at this sort of manipulation and marveled at his own ability to bend crowds to his will. "His success as a demagogue," Ian Kernshaw points out,

lay in his ability to say what the disaffected masses wanted to hear, to speak their language—to capture and exploit a psychology of despair and invest it with new hope for a phoenix-like resurgence [i.e., a rise from the ashes] of the nation. He was able as no one else to give voice to popular hatreds, resentments, hopes, and expectations. He spoke more stridently, more vehemently, more expressively and appealingly than any of

Hitler speaks at a rally in 1934, not long after taking power. Even at a young age, he displayed an uncanny ability to captivate a crowd.

those with a similar ideological message. He was the mouthpiece of the nationalist masses at a decisive time of all-embracing national crises.[23]

What is more, this national crisis that Hitler exploited was not simply about loss and humiliation. The Germans faced some very real and serious economic problems in the years immediately following the Great War, problems that the well-meaning but weak postwar government failed to solve. In November 1918, with total defeat imminent, the leaders of the German Social Democratic Party had proclaimed the country a republic, which became known as the Weimar Republic after the town in which they drew up its constitution. William (or Wilhelm) II, the former kaiser (emperor), soon afterward left the country and abdicated; this opened the way for Germany to join the United States, Britain, and other great and prosperous modern democracies.

But the economic hardships Germany faced in the wake of the war made prosperity, at least for the foreseeable future, an impossible dream. The heavy war reparations imposed by the Allies, combined with the country's already huge debts and the fact that its paper money was not backed by gold, caused horrendous inflation. In 1923, at the height of the economic crisis, 1 billion marks (the mark was

Six Weeks' Pay for a Pair of Boots

From his book Modern Germany, *Koppel S. Pinson, a noted scholar of German history, provides some of the startling facts and figures of German inflation in the early 1920s.*

The inflation left havoc and distress among the workers and especially among the middle classes. Soaring prices far outdistanced increases in wages, and there were resulting strikes and unemployment. Workers had to pay the equivalent of nine to ten hours of work for a pound of margarine, several days' work for a pound of butter, six weeks' pay for a pair of boots, and twenty weeks' pay for a suit of clothes. The most disastrous effects of inflation, however, were felt by the urban middle classes, especially fixed income groups and those living on savings and pensions. These classes suffered economic and psychic damage that left permanent injuries to the social body of Weimar Germany.

Germany's main unit of currency) were needed to equal the buying power of just one prewar mark! Money became worth so little that it required a large potato sack crammed with paper bills to purchase a pair of shoes. And not surprisingly, millions of people lost their jobs and life savings.

"I Could Speak!"

It was during these desperate years, as the Weimar government earnestly struggled to keep Germany from the brink of complete ruin, that Adolf Hitler began the political activities that would eventually lead him into the corridors of ultimate power. After war's end, he returned to Munich. There he attended meetings of some of the many small political groups that wanted to rid the nation of the democracy they viewed as impotent and useless.

One night in 1919, at a meeting in a run-down tavern, Hitler found himself drawn to one of these groups, the German Workers' Party, which at the time had only six members. Later he wrote how "the conviction grew in me that through just such a little movement the rise of the nation could some day be organized." After thinking it over for two days, he recalled, he finally decided to join. "It was the most decisive resolve of my life. From here there was and could be no turning back. And so I registered as a member of the German Workers' Party and received a provi-

sional membership card with the number 7."[24]

For a while the group was unable to attract any more new members. "We were always the same faces," Hitler later wrote. In meetings, "first we received the brotherly greetings, and we were informed that the 'seeds' [of their ideas] had been planted in respective places, or even established and . . . the necessity was stressed to act as a unit."[25] In an attempt to gather prospective recruits, the group placed an ad in an anti-Semitic newspaper, saying that a rally would be held in a cellar room on October 16, 1919. More than seventy people showed up, and Hitler, the main speaker, put on an impressive show. He ranted on and on for more than half an hour, denouncing and threatening Jews, Communists, democrats, and other perceived enemies; and when at last he received a loud ovation from the onlookers, he was elated. "What before I had simply felt deep down in my heart, without being able to put it to the test," he later remembered, "proved to be true; I could speak!"[26]

That night proved to be a foreshadowing of things to come. Following the appointment of the enthusiastic and diligent Hitler to the post of party propaganda officer, the group became better organized and began drawing many new members. In April 1920, at his insistence, it changed its name to the National Socialist German Workers' Party, or NSDAP. (The letters stood

Remembering the Young Hitler

In this tract (quoted in Jeremy Noakes's and Geoffrey Pridham's Documents on Nazism*), noted German historian Karl von Muller recalls meeting the youthful Adolf Hitler at a gathering at a friend's house early in 1923. At this time the Nazi Party, which Hitler headed, was still a relatively small and unimportant political organization.*

My foreboding about Hitler grew only slowly and uncertainly. The second time I met him was peaceful enough. It was for coffee at Erna Hanfstaengl's at the request of Abbot Alban Schachleiter who wanted to meet him; my wife and I were domestic decoration. The four of us had already sat down round the polished mahogany table by the window when the bell rang. Through the open door we could see him greeting his hostess in the narrow passage with almost obsequious politeness, putting down his riding whip, taking off his velour hat and trenchcoat and finally unbuckling a belt with a revolver and hanging it on a peg. It looked comic and reminded me of Karl May [a popular German writer of adventure stories, particularly about the Wild West]. None of us knew then how minutely all these little details in dress and manner were calculated for their effect, just like his striking short trimmed moustache which was narrower than his unattractive broad nose. The man who entered was no longer the stubborn and gauche instructor in a badly fitting uniform who had stood before me in 1919. His look expressed awareness of public success; but a peculiar gaucherie [crudeness] still remained, and one had the uncomfortable feeling that he was conscious of it and resented its being noticed. His face was still thin and pale with an expression almost of suffering. But his protruding pale blue eyes stared at times with a ruthless severity and above his nose between the eyebrows was concentrated a fanatical willpower. On this occasion too he spoke little and for most of the time listened with great attention.

for Nationalsozialistische Deutsche Arbeiterpartei, which translates into English as National Socialist German Workers' Party.) The term Nazi was a convenient abbreviation of the German words for National Socialist. By July 1921, when Hitler became the group's supreme leader, Nazi membership stood at about six thousand; in the next two years, aided in no small degree by the party's own right-wing newspaper, the *Munich Observer*, that number mushroomed to fifty-five thousand.

During this period Hitler also established the *Sturmabteilung*, or "storm troopers," known more simply as the SA, basically strong-arm men who guarded him, patrolled party meetings, and carried out various acts of violence and intimidation at his orders. The storm troopers were led by Ernst Röhm, who had worked as a political adviser to local German infantry units. They wore brown shirts (prompting their nickname, the "Brownshirts") and carried weapons.

The armbands sported by the storm troopers bore the new Nazi emblem, the swastika, a mystic symbol of ancient origin. (The swastika has been found in the ruins of ancient Troy, in what is now Turkey, as well as among ancient Egyptian and Chinese artifacts. In modern times prior to Hitler's rise, the Baltic states of Estonia and Finland used it as a battle emblem.

Various anti-Semitic German political groups then adopted it before Hitler made it nationally and internationally famous, or, perhaps more properly, infamous.) The symbol's four crooked arms supposedly indicated the four directions of the earth, implying world conquest, and also stood for the party's violent anti-Semitism. The party's flag (which eventually became Germany's flag) showed a black swastika in a white disk, the disk surrounded by a bright red background. "As National Socialists, we see our program in our flag," Hitler later declared.

In *red* we see the social idea of the movement, in *white* the nationalistic

idea, and in the *swastika* the mission of the struggle for the victory of the Aryan man . . . [which] has been and always will be anti-Semitic" (the italics are Hitler's).[27]

Hitler's Ideas and Speaking Techniques

Beyond this and other ambiguous references to "national struggles" against Jews, Communists, and liberal democratic institutions, it is difficult to isolate and analyze Nazi doctrine, that is, its system of principles and beliefs. It is clear that from the beginning Hitler and his followers wanted to take over the national government. But aside from that tactical goal, as Erich Kahler points out, National Socialism was based more on the use of force to get its way than on any clear-cut or original ideology (set of ideas).

Although Nazism embodied principles that had long been at work in Western society, it certainly cannot be considered an ideological movement like socialism [or] Communism. . . . Despite its ideological slogans proclaiming a new order in a new Europe, National Socialism never had the slightest awareness of its true function in human history. In and of itself it was nothing but a criminal conspiracy of national and international proportions. . . . Nazism did not hesitate to appropriate anything that could serve its purpose, perverting ideas and ideologies only to discard them when they had outlasted their usefulness. But National Socialism had no ideas or ideology of its own . . . or to put it another way, its ideological basis was pure hoax. The Nazi state did not operate on principle but on tactics. . . . The only lasting "principles" in the Nazi bag of tricks were racism, anti-Christianism, and anti-humanitarianism, all of which had permanent value as means of destroying the moral judgment of the population.[28]

Relying on this "bag of tricks" as an orator at the early Nazi Party meetings,

This widely publicized series of photos of Hitler speaking at a rally shows the range of facial expressions and hand gestures he employed in his own oratory.

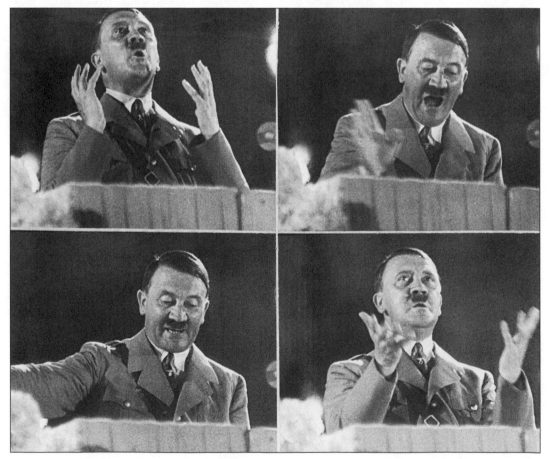

Hitler demonstrated his ability to hold an audience spellbound. Although wartime mustard gas had scarred his vocal cords, making his voice harsh and raspy, he possessed a natural charisma and emotional intensity that made people pay attention to him. He also worked hard at mastering the art of delivery. He used his arms and hands very expressively, as remembered by a follower, Ernst Hanfstaengl: "It had something of the quality of a really great orchestral conductor who instead of just hammering out the downward beat, suggests the existence of hidden rhythms and meaning with the upward flick of his baton." Hitler also injected no small amount of theatrics into his speeches. He often interrupted himself, Hanfstaengl says, "with a counter-argument and then [returned] to his original line of thought after completely annihilating his supposed adversary."[29]

Another effective speaking technique Hitler employed was first to play on his listeners' emotions and then to connect them in a personal way directly to the thematic material of the speech. He told Hanfstaengl in private:

When I talk to people, especially those who are not yet Party members . . . I always talk as if the fate of the nation was bound up in their decision. . . . Certainly it means appealing to their vanity and ambition, but once I have got them to that point, the rest is easy.

Slumbering somewhere [within them] is the readiness to risk some final sacrifice, some adventure, in order to give a new shape to their lives. They will spend their last money on a lottery ticket. It is my business to channel that urge for political purposes. . . . The humbler people are, the greater craving to identify themselves with a cause bigger than themselves, and if I can persuade them that the fate of the German nation is at stake, then they will become part of an irresistible movement, embracing all classes.[30]

These remarks show clearly that, despite the image he projected of a man who cared for and wanted to help the people, Hitler actually held the German masses in contempt. In one of his more notable such expressions, he compared the people as a whole to women, whom he also viewed as ignorant inferiors who must ultimately submit absolutely to his will:

Like a woman whose psychic feeling is influenced less by abstract reasoning than by indefinable sentimental longing for complementary strength, who will submit to the strong man rather than dominate the weakling, thus the masses love the ruler rather than the suppliant. . . . They neither realize the impudence with which they are spiritually terrorized nor the outrageous curtailment of their human liberties, for in no way does the delusion of this doctrine dawn on them. Thus they see only the inconsiderate force, the brutality and the aim of its manifestations to which they finally always submit.[31]

The Führer's Failed Coup

In these early years of National Socialism's struggle, Hitler's speeches also sometimes provoked extreme reactions.

On a number of occasions, his audiences became so impassioned that fights erupted between his supporters and those who disliked his ideas. And such detractors were numerous, for his agenda and personal manner were so outrageous that at first many people laughed at him and refused to take him or the Nazis seriously. Indeed, some were sure that he was mentally unbalanced. One such observer was Fredrich Reck-Malleczewen, a well-to-do German businessman who described meeting Hitler at the house of a friend in 1920:

Do You Want to Be Jewish Slaves?

These are excerpts from a 1920 pamphlet (quoted in Simon Taylor's Rise of Hitler*) written by Anton Drexler, one of Hitler's colleagues in the group that would soon become the Nazi Party. This is a clear example of how the group used racist fantasies and distortions to appeal to anti-Jewish feelings that were widespread in Munich and other German cities at the time.*

There is a secret world conspiracy, which while speaking much about humanity and tolerance, in reality wants only to harness the people to a new yoke. A number of workers' leaders belong to this group. The leaders are big capitalists. . . . 300 big bankers, financiers and press barons, who are interconnected across the world, are the real dictators. They belong almost exclusively to the "chosen people." They are all members of this same secret conspiracy, which organizes world politics. . . . Their aim is: THE DICTATORSHIP OF MONEY OVER WORK. . . . When will we finally see through the false friends of our movement? The Jewish big capitalist always plays our friend and do-gooder; but he only does it to make us into his slaves. The trusting worker is going to help him to set up the world dictatorship of Jewry. Because that is their goal, as it states in the Bible. "All the peoples will serve you, all the wealth of the world will belong to you." . . . In the Talmud it says, 'a time is coming when every Jew will have 2800 slaves: Comrades, do you want to be Jewish slaves?

Hitler (fourth from right) stands with fellow collaborators in the infamous Beer Hall Putsch. The coup failed to launch him into power.

A jelly-like, slag-gray face, a moon-face into which two melancholy jet-black eyes had been set like raisins. So sad, so unutterably insignificant, so basically misbegotten. . . . He had come to a house, where he had never been before, wearing gaiters [leather lower-leg coverings], a floppy, wide-brimmed hat, and carrying a riding whip. . . . Eventually, he managed to launch into a speech. He talked on and on, endlessly. He preached. He went on at us like a division Chaplain in the Army. We did not in the least contradict him, or venture to differ in any way, but he began to bellow at us. The servants thought we were being attacked, and rushed in to defend us. . . . When he had gone, we sat silently confused. . . . There was a feeling of dismay, as when on a train you suddenly find you are sharing a compartment with a psychotic. . . . It was not that an unclean body had been in the room, but something else: the unclean essence of a monstrosity.[32]

Reck-Malleczewen and others who did not take Hitler seriously were likely surprised when he made his first major bid for power late in 1923, in what is known as the Beer Hall Putsch (coup). On the night of November 8, some three thousand senior state officials and military men held a meeting at the Bürgerbräukeller, a large beer hall on the southern outskirts of Munich. After Hitler's SA troops surrounded the building, he suddenly burst into the hall, jumped up on a table, and fired a pistol into the air. "The National Revolution has begun!" he shouted.

Meanwhile, Röhm led other SA units in a takeover of Munich's army headquarters. But within a day their daring putsch failed, after senior army generals in Berlin ordered police and army personnel in the Munich area to suppress the Nazis. The authorities promptly arrested Hitler and dissolved the National Socialist Party. The führer, or supreme leader, as he had come to call himself, went to trial in February 1924 and on April 1 received a sentence of five years in prison.

Government officials likely thought they had seen the last of Adolf Hitler

Shortly after the failed Beer Hall Putsch, Hitler (left) strikes a defiant pose along with his cronies Maurice Kriebel, Rudolph Hess, and Max Weber.

and his brutal thugs. But the arrogant closing speech he delivered at the trial, in which he warned that he and his followers would rise again, would, sadly for Germany and the world, turn out to be prophetic. "The army which we have formed grows from day to day," the Nazi demagogue began.

From hour to hour it grows more rapidly. Even now I have the proud hope that one day the hour is coming when these untrained bands will become battalions, when the battalions will become regiments and the regiments divisions, when the old cockade [revolutionary badge, often worn on a hat] will be raised from the mire, when the old banners will once again wave before us; and then reconciliation will come in that eternal last Court of Judgment—the Court of God—before which we are ready to take our stand.

Then from our bones, from our graves will sound the voice of that tribunal which alone has the right to sit in judgment upon us. For, gentlemen, it is not you who pronounce judgment upon us, it is the eternal Court of History which will make its pronouncement upon the charge which is brought against us. The judgment that you will pass, that I know. But that Court will not ask of us "Have you committed high treason or not?" That Court will judge us . . . who as Germans have wished the best for their people and their Fatherland, who wished to fight and to die. You may declare us guilty a thousand times, but the Goddess who presides over the Eternal Court of History will with a smile tear in pieces the charge of the Public Prosecutor and the judgment of the court, for she declares us guiltless.[33]

Chapter Three

1923–1933: TRIUMPH OF THE WILL

Unfortunately for Germany and the world, rather than relegating Hitler to obscurity, his stay in prison only strengthened him and made him more dangerous. First, that stay was relatively short; because he was eligible for early parole, he served only nine months of his five-year sentence. More significantly, these months constituted a pivotal period both for him and the German nation, for it was in his prison cell that he penned much of his famous volume, *Mein Kampf,* meaning "My Struggle." (Hitler originally titled the book "Four and a Half Years of Struggle Against Lies, Stupidity and Cowardice"; but his publisher informed him that such a long and ponderous title would not sell and insisted that he shorten it to the simpler and stronger "My Struggle.")

The book combines accounts of Hitler's life up to the time of the Beer Hall Putsch with tracts outlining his political and viciously anti-Semitic views and distorted interpretations of German and world history. From a literary standpoint, the writing is unoriginal, pompous, repetitive, disorganized, often inconsistent, and at times decidedly irrational. These weaknesses made (and still make) the volume extremely difficult to read and understand. Yet it sold millions of copies and became the gospel of Nazism. It also gave Hitler, whom so many people had laughed at in the past, a kind of pseudo-intellectual respectability in the eyes of the German public.

This image of respectability slowly but steadily translated into one of political legitimacy for a public that had once seen Hitler as a squalid little fanatic on the fringes of society. Indeed, Hitler had come to realize that power could not be achieved without such legitimacy, and legitimacy could not be achieved from society's extremist sidelines. He had learned his lesson from the failed coup and now recast the Nazis as loyal Germans willing to promote their views within the existing system. This approach would take longer, of course, to achieve the desired goal—a Nazi dictatorship. But Hitler was willing to be patient because he was confident of ultimate victory. He saw the German masses (and those of other lands, too) as "weak and bestial," "as stupid as they are forgetful," and "lazy and cowardly."[34] As such, they could not hope to improve their own

How the Jews Twist the Truth

In this excerpt from his Mein Kampf, *Hitler claims that Jews purposely lie and states that this is one of the reasons he had come to hate them.*

The more I argued with them, the better I came to know their dialectic [method of argument]. First they counted on the stupidity of their adversary, and then, when there was no other way out, they themselves simply played stupid. If all this didn't help, they pretended not to understand, or, if challenged, they changed the subject in a hurry, quoted platitudes which, if you accepted them, they immediately related to entirely different matters, and then, if again attacked, gave ground and pretended not to know exactly what you were talking about. Whenever you tried to attack one of these apostles, your hand closed on a jelly-like slime which divided up and poured through your fingers, but in the next moment collected again. But if you really struck one of these fellows so telling a blow that, observed by the audience, he couldn't help but agree, and if you believed that this had taken you at least one step forward, your amazement was great the next day. The Jew had not the slightest recollection of the day before, he rattled off his same old nonsense as though nothing at all had happened, and, if indignantly challenged, affected amazement; he couldn't remember a thing, except that he had proved the correctness of his assertions the previous day. Sometimes I stood there thunderstruck. I didn't know what to be more amazed at: the agility of their tongues or their virtuosity at lying. Gradually I began to hate them.

lot all by themselves. Instead, he reasoned, in their ignorance and aimlessness, they were searching for a new national hero to unify them and give them direction and purpose. In Hitler's mind, as Ian Kernshaw puts it:

> Hopes could be invested only in the vision of such a hero—warrior, statesman, and high priest rolled into one—who would arise from the ashes of national humiliation and post-war misery to restore national pride and greatness. The seeds of subsequent intellectual backing for Hitler and his movement were fertilized in such soil—however distant reality proved to be from the ideal.[35]

From that soil, Hitler succeeded in growing a mighty tree; his plan to place himself at the reins of the German government took less than ten years to implement. These were difficult years for him and his followers. Yet he remained resolute, ever guided by his own warped sense of self-importance and by his demented, evil blueprint for the acquisition and application of absolute power—*Mein Kampf.*

Laying Out Nazi Ideals and Goals

Most importantly, a number of the ideas Hitler discussed in the book appealed to millions of Germans who felt betrayed by the "stab in the back" and who were presently suffering from the economic ravages of the postwar inflation. Themes he harped on often included the Jews' "inferiority" and "dishonesty" and the "unfair" treatment of Germany by the Allies and international bankers. He made it clear that he and Germany would get their just revenge on all of these groups. France, for example, would be made to suffer for its arrogant treatment of the Germans during and after World War I. "The inexorable mortal enemy of the German people," France would eventually succumb to Germany in "a last decisive struggle."[36]

This idea of getting back at the French appealed strongly to most Germans, as did Hitler's emphasis on the supposed superiority of the Aryan race (and by contrast, the subhuman status of the Jews, Poles, Slavs, and many others). Throughout history, he held (without offering any evidence, of course, since none existed), the Aryans had been the rightful masters. But they had often made the unforgivable mistake of diluting their blood through intermarriage with inferior peoples. "Blood mixture," he insisted,

> and the resultant drop in the racial level is the sole cause of the dying out of old cultures; for men do not perish as a result of lost wars, but by the loss of that force of resistance which is contained only in pure blood. All who are not of good race in this world are chaff [refuse or waste material].[37]

Endorsing the Big Lie

Hitler's Mein Kampf, *like its author, is filled with inconsistencies and contradictions. One of the most striking is his rabid denunciation of the Jews as liars, followed by this passage endorsing his own political use of the "big lie" to control the populace.*

In the size of the lie there is always contained a certain factor of credibility, since the great masses of people ... will more easily fall victim to a great lie than to a small one, since they themselves ... lie sometimes in little things. ... Thus such an untruth will not at all enter their heads. ... Therefore, just for this reason, some part of the most impudent lie will remain and stick.

Only through maintaining racial purity, therefore, could the remaining Aryans hope to regain their mastery over the earth.

Of particular appeal to many Germans was Hitler's discussion of *Lebensraum*—"living space," a theme that obsessed him for the rest of his life. In his view, Germany's future hinged on its forceful seizure of European lands, into which German settlers could expand, live comfortably, and propagate more superior Aryans. The most suitable territories, he said bluntly, were the Russian steppes, which must first be cleared of inferior peoples, especially the Slavs. "Let us be given soil we need for our livelihood," he wrote.

True, they [the displaced peoples] will not willingly do this. But then the law of self-preservation goes into effect; and what is refused to amicable methods, it is up to the fist to take. ... If land was desired in Europe, it could be obtained, by and large, only at the expense of Russia, and this means that the new Reich must again set itself on the march along the road of the Teutonic Knights of old [Germans who invaded Russia in the thirteenth century], to obtain by the German sword sod for the German plow and daily bread for the nation.[38]

These goals of punishing enemy nations, mastering and ruling inferior peoples, and acquiring living space, Hitler wrote, could be and should be achieved in only one way—naked, brutal force. This method lay at the core of

Weltanschauung, his crude philosophical worldview, which stressed a simplistic sort of Darwinian "law of the jungle." Only the fittest were worthy of surviving, he maintained, and ruling a "world where one creature feeds on the other and where the death of the weaker implies the life of the stronger." Furthermore, he insisted, "Those who want to live, let them fight, and those who do not want to fight . . . do not deserve to live. . . . That is how it is!"[39]

Obstacles in Hitler's Path

Although *Mein Kampf* touched a nerve with many Germans, its effect was far from revolutionary and Hitler's public popularity and influence grew only gradually in the years following his release from prison. On the one hand, many Germans wanted to give the weak but still promising Weimar democracy a chance to prove itself. On the other, the Nazis' botched 1923 coup had shown Hitler that the strong-arm approach was, at least for the present, dangerous and unrealistic; to gain governmental power, he now realized, the newly reestablished National Socialists would have to work within the existing system as a legitimate political party.

This was not an easy proposition, if for no other reason than that the Nazi movement had been severely weakened by the failed 1923 coup and Hitler's imprisonment. After he was released, the governments of various German provinces banned him from speaking in public. Moreover, another right-wing demagogue, Gregor Strasser, had begun to build up a rival Nazi power center in northern Germany. Strasser agreed with a proposal of the Social Democrats and Communists that the government should seize and divide up the lucrative estates and private fortunes of the German nobles who had fallen from power at the end of the Great War. This infuriated Hitler. Members of former noble families had controlling interests in many key German industries; and a number of these industries, which had right-wing political leanings, had earlier shown an interest in backing Hitler. He knew that his own Nazi organization could not succeed without the backing of these industrialists.

Over the course of about five years, Hitler managed to eliminate most of these obstacles. In February 1926 he won over Strasser's chief Nazi supporter, Joseph Goebbels (GER-blz), and neutralized Strasser's independent influence within the Nazi Party. Goebbels became the party's propaganda chief, while Hitler gathered around him other hardcore lieutenants, including Hermann Göring, who would later become his right-hand man and commander of Germany's air force; Heinrich Himmler, who would lead the dreaded Nazi secret police; and Julius Streicher, a vehement anti-Semitic journalist. These men and their subordinates worked tirelessly to get the Nazis' message out to the

Hitler presides over the official founding of the Nazi party in Munich in 1925. Rival Nazi leader Gregor Strasser sits at Hitler's left.

German people. They were aided by a lifting of the bans on Hitler's public speeches in 1927 and 1928. And in the following two years, several large industrialists began to funnel money into the Nazi Party; they hoped that if Hitler was elected to high office, he would support their own anti-working-class (and therefore anti-liberal and anti-democratic) agenda.

A New Political Approach

Despite these positive gains, at first the Nazis fared poorly in national elections.

41

In the 1928 election, for instance, they received less than 3 percent of the national vote. This was due largely to the fact that Weimar Germany underwent a period of increasing economic recovery in the late 1920s. However, the worldwide effects of the Great Depression initiated by the crash of the New York stock market in 1929 delivered the new German economy a sudden and catastrophic blow. Thrown back into bitterness and despair, the German people increasingly came to support right-wing parties that promised

Four of Hitler's top henchmen. Clockwise from top left: Hermann Göering, Julius Streicher, Joseph Goebbels, and Heinrich Himmler.

a quick fix for the nation's problems. More and more, Hitler's messages reached wider sections of the population. Moreover, he had learned to project a milder, less threatening image than the one he had as a young political agitator. His speeches now appealed to the real needs of the average German, even if his toned-down rhetoric masked his truly radical plans for the country. "It was clear to him," one observer noted,

> that he could only win the attention of the masses by avoiding the usual [extreme right-wing] terminology and working with new words and new conceptions. His train of thought was of such generally compelling nature that people of different political directions could agree with it. So during his first public appearance in Hamburg, he was able, within a single hour, to persuade a suspicious and reserved audience to applaud, and this applause increased until it became . . . an enthusiastic ovation. Later, the most level-headed listeners declared that . . . Hitler . . . was obviously much more reasonable than they had imagined.[40]

One of the many examples of Hitler's donning the guise of a legitimate and reasonable politician was a speech he gave at a beer hall in 1930.

Albert Speer was there and later recalled how the Nazi leader captivated the audience:

> Hitler entered and was tempestuously hailed by his numerous followers among the students. This enthusiasm in itself made a great impression upon me. But his appearance also surprised me. On posters and in caricatures I had seen him in military tunic, with shoulder straps, swastika armband, and hair flapping over his forehead. But here he was wearing a well-fitted blue suit and looking markedly respectable. Everything about him bore out the note of reasonable modesty. Later I learned that he had a great gift for adjusting—consciously—or intuitively—to his surroundings. . . . In a low voice, hesitantly and somewhat shyly, he began a kind of historical lecture rather than a speech. To me there was something engaging about it—all the more so since it ran counter to everything the propaganda of his opponents had led me to expect: a hysterical demagogue, a shrieking and gesticulating fanatic in uniform. . . . It seemed as if he were candidly presenting his anxieties about the future. His irony was softened by a somewhat self-conscious humor; his South German charm reminded me agreeably

Hitler delivers an election speech in 1932. President Paul von Hindenburg beat Hitler in the election.

of my native region. . . . He spoke urgently and with hypnotic persuasiveness. The mood he cast was much deeper than the speech itself, most of which I did not remember for long. Moreover, I was carried on the wave of the enthusiasm which, one could almost feel this physically, bore the speaker along from sentence to sentence. It swept away any skepticism, any reservations.[41]

Victory Over the System

As a result of Hitler's persistent, calculated political efforts, the National Socialist Party steadily gained appeal and electoral power. In the 1930 election for seats in the Reichstag, the German parliament, the Nazis received an impressive 18 percent of the vote, which translated into 107 seats. Two years later, the term of office of the country's weak and aged president, Paul von Hindenburg, expired, necessitating a presidential election. (Under the Weimar Republic's constitution, the president served for seven years.) Hitler, who emerged as Hindenburg's leading opponent, garnered 30 percent of the vote. Although Hindenburg beat him by a wide margin, no single candidate gained a clear majority, so a run-off election was held a month later; Hindenburg won again, but this time Hitler's share of the vote increased to almost 37 percent.

In July 1932 Franz von Papen, the new chancellor (prime minister of the presidential cabinet, in charge of formulating national policies), called a new Reichstag election. He hoped that the Nazis would lose ground and therefore end up playing only a small role in the government. But to his surprise, the Nazis won 230 seats in the parliament, becoming the nation's largest single party. Hitler now demanded the chancellorship. Neither Hindenburg nor Papen wanted to see him in that powerful office; but after much political intriguing and maneuvering by both sides, they came to believe that they could make him chancellor and then dominate and control him.

These politicians had sorely underestimated the Nazi leader, however. Immediately after Hindenburg appointed him chancellor on January 30, 1933, Hitler swiftly and ruthlessly initiated a series of moves designed to give him dictatorial powers. First, he temporarily dissolved the Reichstag and called for new elections. During the campaign, Nazi storm troopers intimidated and terrorized opposing candidates and denied them the use of radio and the press. In the meantime, a Communist agitator played right into Hitler's hands by setting fire to the Reichstag building. Fearing a rash of similar terrorist incidents, and urged on by Hitler, Hindenburg issued emergency decrees suspending free speech and press, which made it even easier for Nazi storm troopers to spread their own brand of terror.

The end result of this series of events was telling. Although the Nazis did not achieve a majority of votes in the election, their 44 percent share was enough. When the new Reichstag convened on March 23, 1933, all non-Nazi members, under threat of retaliation by the SA, voted with the Nazis for the Enabling Act. This law suspended the Weimar constitution and conferred dictatorial powers on the government, thereby giving birth to the Third

In this photo taken on September 4, 1933, five months after the passage of the Enabeling Act, Hitler sits with Hindenburg during a national celebration.

Reich. (Hitler reckoned the medieval Germanic Holy Roman Empire as the First Reich and the German union forged in 1871 by Otto von Bismarck as the Second Reich. As leader of the so-called "Third Reich," Hitler portrayed himself as the successor to Germany's great past leaders and, for attacking the forces that had humiliated and destroyed the "glorious" Second Reich, the country's savior.)

Hitler justified the Enabling Act in a speech delivered on April 5, 1933, assuring the German people that they would continue to have a voice in deciding their own destiny. "Owing to the Enabling Act," he began,

the work of the deliverance of the German people has been freed and released for the first time from the party views and considerations of our former representative assembly. With its assistance we shall now be able to do what, after clear-sighted examination and dispassionate consideration, appears necessary for the future of the nation. The purely legislative previous conditions necessary for this have been provided. But it is also necessary that the people itself should take an active part in this action. The nation must not

Hitler (standing at the lectern) speaks to Hindenburg (seated at lower right) after being sworn in as Germany's chancellor early in 1933.

A Hymn of Praise to Hitler

One of the tools Hitler effectively used to promote his image and that of Nazism was the motion picture. Beginning in the late 1920s, German cinema became increasingly right wing in its themes; and when the Nazis came to power, they were careful to exploit films for propaganda purposes—especially in short films and newsreels. No motion picture did more to glorify and solidify Hitler's image than *Triumph of the Will*, directed by his favorite filmmaker, Leni Riefenstahl. Set in a vast Nazi Party rally staged at Nuremburg in 1934, the film depicts, in a highly dramatic and romantic style, Hitler marching through enormous massed ranks of soldiers and other followers and speaking to them. Noted film historian Roger Manville calls it (in *Films and the Second World War*) "an emotional hymn of praise to Hitler." In a repulsive display of egotism and self-gratification, the führer had commissioned the film himself. He had even chosen the title, which he felt appropriately summed up the personal talents and inner fortitude that had allowed him to rise from humble beginnings to the heights of power in the 1920s and early 1930s.

Nazis rally at Nuremburg in 1934 in a scene from the film *Triumph of the Will*. At left with Hitler is the director, Leni Riefenstahl.

imagine that, because the Reichstag can no more restrict our decisions, the nation itself no longer needs to take part in the shaping of our destiny. On the contrary, we wish that the German people at this very time should concentrate once more and cooperate actively in support of the Government. The result must be that when we appeal to the nation once more, in four years' time, we shall not appeal to men who have been asleep, but will find ourselves faced by a nation that has finally awakened in the course of these years from its parliamentary trance and has realized the knowledge necessary to understand the eternal conditions of human existence.[42]

This pledge to allow the German people to decide their own destiny would quickly prove as false as other Nazi promises of justice and fair play. Now that his long struggle for ultimate power in Germany had at last been crowned with success, Hitler no longer had to worry about fair play or working within the system. What the German people did not yet know was that the Nazis had won a victory *over* rather than *under* the existing system. In Hitler's own quite immoderate view, that victory had been a triumph of his superior will over diverse negative forces that had long sought to destroy or restrain him. Not long after gaining power, he called on a noted German filmmaker, Leni Riefenstahl, to commemorate this concept, as well as his political victory, in a documentary with the appropriate and catchy title of *Triumph of the Will*. Hitler would now begin to enforce that will with whatever means he deemed necessary as he transformed the country to meet his distorted personal vision.

Chapter Four

1933–1939:
A Nation
Transformed

Hindenburg, Papen, and other more moderate German leaders had grossly underestimated Hitler's public appeal, political abilities, and, most of all, his iron resolve. As the leaders of other Western nations would be later, they were surprised by the degree to which the Nazi chief took himself and his rhetoric seriously. Almost none of them expected him actually to implement his most extreme ideas; after all, they were quite used to politicians saying whatever was needed to get elected but largely maintaining the status quo once in office. More than any other single factor, this miscalculation had been the key to Hitler's success. In Robert Waite's words, his opponents had misunderstood and misread him

because they thought (quite rightly) that his ideas were ridiculous and beneath contempt. They failed to realize that Hitler believed in those ideas. They greatly overestimated his opportunistic and manipulative side and underestimated his commitment to ideology. It is of the utmost importance to emphasize that Hitler was a man both of *contrivance* and conviction, an *opportunist* and a fanatic. . . . The horror of Hitler was this: he meant what he said, he lived by his ideals, he practiced what he preached.[43]

It soon became abundantly clear that Hitler had indeed meant what he had said. In the first months of his chancellorship, he swiftly went about the business of eradicating democracy altogether and turning Germany into a police state tightly controlled by the Nazis. Most high-placed and influential Germans, even many traditional conservatives, were disturbed by these events. But once Hitler and his strong-arm men were in power, it was too late. His public image and military backing were too compelling to dislodge, except by a rival faction of equal strength; and

The Reichstag Building burns in February 1933. Hitler later used the incident to bolster his power.

no such faction then existed in Germany. Opponents of Nazism could only watch in dismay as Hitler steadily transformed the nation, building on and exploiting racist and warlike tendencies that had already long existed in German society.

Powers of the Secret Police

From the beginning, Hitler recognized that such a transformation could not be accomplished without enforcers who could both instill fear and keep order. The job of enforcing Nazi policies and maintaining control over the populace fell on an elite and "racially pure" force of honor guards, the SS (the *Schutzstaffel*, or "defense corps," also called the "Black-shirts"), led by the ruthless Heinrich Himmler. Using a special branch of the SS, the Gestapo, or secret police, Himmler effectively employed terror tactics to root out and often to torture and kill those opposed to Nazism.

Not surprisingly, such abuses against German citizens were against the law at the time that Hitler came to power. But he quickly remedied this situation. Thanks to Hindenburg's knee-jerk reaction to the Reichstag fire crisis in February 1933, many guarantees of civil

---

Hitler Gains the Army's Support

In this excerpt from Hitler in History, *German historian Eberhard Jäckel explains how Hitler ensured the all-important support of the German army after achieving national power in the 1930s.*

The relationship between Hitler and the army was not easy, its support never a matter of course. He won its support from one juncture to the next only by flattering and obliging its leaders and not least by corrupting them. He corrupted them personally by cash awards and grand decorations, but above all and principally by making them his accomplices. This happened for the first time during the liquidation of [Ernst] Röhm [head of the SA, or Brownshirts], in which the army took an active part. But it soon became a favorite technique that he used on many other occasions. Hitler did not like to rely on friends who shared his views, and, indeed, he had almost no friends. Instead he relied on accomplices whom he had so corrupted that they could no longer desert him. He liked people to burn their bridges behind them. That was the kind of loyalty he understood.

liberties had already been suspended. In the following three years, the government exploited this situation by issuing various decrees that made the secret police, in effect, above the law and answerable only to the führer himself. One leading Gestapo officer, Werner Best, remarked, "As long as the police carries out the will of the leadership, it is acting legally."[44]

Utilizing the dreaded SS Blackshirts, Hitler and Himmler wasted no time in initiating a veritable reign of terror. The secret police arrested thousands of citizens, Jew and non-Jew alike, often on mere suspicion of being against the new regime. And by the end of 1933, only months after Hitler had come to power, about fifty concentration camps had been erected to house these detainees. (Most of the camps were originally run by Röhm's SA.) In these facilities, many prisoners were brutally tortured and some were murdered by sadistic SS guards simply for sport. In another common practice, the organization ransomed prisoners to their families and pocketed the money. The severity of treatment in these camps explains in part why the SS was so effective in keeping the public in line. Two regulations put in place at the camp at Dachau in November 1933 are chillingly illustrative:

Article 11. The following offenders, considered as agitators, will be hanged: Anyone who . . . politicizes, holds inciting speeches and meetings, forms cliques, loiters around with others; who for the purpose of supplying the propaganda of the opposition with atrocity stories, collects true or false information about the concentration camp; receives such information, buries it, talks about it to others, smuggles it out of the camp into the hands of foreign visitors, etc.

Article 12. The following offenders, considered as mutineers, will be shot on the spot or later hanged: Anyone attacking physically a guard or SS man, refusing to obey or to work while on detail . . . or bawling, shouting, inciting or holding speeches while marching or at work.[45]

The sweeping powers of the SS and its importance to Hitler inevitably put both on a collision course with Röhm's SA, the führer's original band of enforcers, which had grown extremely large and powerful in recent years. Many SA members expected to be handed prime positions of power in the Reich in return for helping Hitler rise to power. When he did not so reward them, some became disgruntled, and Hitler, now seeing them as a threat to his new order, decided to eliminate them. On June 30, 1934, the führer himself led the "blood purge," the so-called "Night of the Long Knives," in which as many as one thousand SA

In this Nazi concentration camp, known as Stalag 4, the guards starved and then burned some four hundred Russian, French, and Jewish political prisoners.

leaders, including Röhm, were arrested and executed. Years later the warden of Munich's Stradelheim prison recalled how the once powerful Röhm met his end:

Two SS men asked at the reception desk to be taken to Röhm. . . . [In the cell] they handed over a Browning [revolver] to Röhm, who once again asked to speak to Hitler. They ordered him to shoot himself. If he did not comply they would come back in ten minutes and kill him. . . . When the time was up, the two SS men reentered the cell, and found Röhm standing with his chest bared. Immediately one of them . . . shot him in the throat, and Röhm collapsed on the floor. Since he was still alive, he was killed with a shot point-blank through the temple.[46]

This naked display of treachery and murder was Röhm's reward for his many years of unswerving loyalty and friendship to Adolf Hitler.

Ernst Röhm (1887–1934), commander of the Nazi storm troopers, met his death when Hitler turned on him.

Society Conforms to Hitler's Views

Meanwhile, using similarly forceful means, the Nazis steadily transformed German society. Public demonstrations were banned. School teachers had to teach Nazi principles and use history texts rewritten to conform to Hitler's distorted version of past events. Even colleges had to follow the party line. Books, theories, and ideas originated by Jews were banned, including Albert Einstein's essential contributions to physics and those of Sigmund Freud to psychology. In a similar vein, art in museums was censored to reflect Hitler's personal tastes; he hated abstract art, for example. The Nazi dictator also passed a law (in July 1933) authorizing the forced sterilization of anyone the regime deemed inferior; included were handicapped people, the mentally ill, alcoholics, prostitutes, and others. A few years later, the führer took this insidious policy a step further by giving verbal orders to begin the wholesale killing of mental patients in German hospitals. When a district judge protested, one of Hitler's lieutenants told him, "If you cannot recognize the will of the führer as a source of law, as a basis of law, then you cannot remain a judge."[47] The judge soon resigned.

At the same time, some 8 million boys and girls between the ages of ten and eighteen were ordered to join the

Hitler Youth movement, which indoctrinated them with National Socialist ideals and instilled in them fanatical devotion for the "beloved Führer." On a single day in the early 1930s, more than a hundred thousand of them crowded into Berlin to hear him speak, after which they marched past him for over seven hours to show their respect and adulation. The reasons why so many young Germans were drawn to Hitler are many and complex. At least in part, Waite suggests, he

responded to their particular, deeply felt psychological needs. He

Thousands of young Germans, members of the Hitler Youth movement, march in Hitler's honor in Berlin in February 1934.

was the incarnation of the idealized father-Führer they had imagined during the disturbing years of their infancy [the economically difficult war and immediate postwar years]; he was what they had always hoped their own fathers would be—"the unknown hero of the trenches" who returned [from the war] in glory. . . . He was a soldier-leader who promised to establish a military state where children and adults would wear military uniforms and march in purposeful, disciplined ranks. They would swear an oath of total fidelity to this deified and distant Führer and help him build a resurgent and powerful German nation.[48]

It is a disturbing testament to Hitler's evil exploitation of an entire generation of innocent young Germans that tens of thousands of them spied on their own parents and reported on the anti-Nazi views of their teachers.

Numerous other aspects of the new German police state were equally disturbing. Both children and adults regularly greeted one other with the Nazi salute (stiffly raising the right arm) and the expression "Heil Hitler!" (Hail Hitler!). The Reich Chamber of Culture, under the propaganda minister, Goebbels, tightly controlled and censored the press, radio, films, and other forms of communication. Goebbels also oversaw the distribution of a steady stream of anti-Semitic and anti-Christian propaganda and the burning of books deemed harmful to Nazism. Not surprisingly, some Christians and most Jews suffered discrimination, persecution, threats, and at times violent attacks.

"Cruelty Is Impressive"

Hitler's persecution of Jews came as no surprise to most people, since years before in *Mein Kampf* he had clearly spelled out the need to "put the Jews in their place." Nazi thugs regularly harassed and beat Jews and/or hauled them away to the concentration camps for torture and questioning; and the vandalizing of Jewish businesses and synagogues became commonplace. These assaults culminated on November 10, 1938, later called *Kristallnacht,* or the "Night of the Broken Glass," in which a frightening wave of anti-Jewish violence swept across Germany. In addition, Jews were increasingly driven out of cultural endeavors such as book publishing, newspaper editing, the arts, theater, and filmmaking. In the following excerpt from a speech delivered on January 30, 1937, Hitler claims that this exclusionary policy had greatly benefited the country:

Consider this fact alone: Our entire German educational system, including the Press, the theatre, films, literature, etc., is today conducted and controlled exclusively by our German fellow-countrymen [i.e.,

The Night of the Broken Glass

This is part of the report (quoted from Jeremy Noakes's and Geoffrey Pridham's Nazism, *1919–1945) filed on November 21, 1938, by David Buffum, the American consul in the German city of Leipzig who witnessed firsthand the terrifying night of anti-Jewish persecution earlier that month.*

At 3 A.M. on 10 November 1938 was unleashed a barrage of Nazi ferocity as had had no equal hitherto [before] in Germany, or very likely anywhere else in the world since savagery began. Jewish buildings were smashed into and contents demolished or looted. In one of the Jewish sections an eighteen-year-old boy was hurled from a three-story window to land with both legs broken on a street littered with burning beds and other household furniture and effects from his family's and other apartments. This information was supplied by an attending physician. It is reported from another quarter that among domestic effects thrown out of a Jewish building, a small dog descended four flights onto a cluttered street with a broken spine. Although apparently centered in poorer districts, the raid was not confined to the humble classes. One apartment of exceptionally refined occupants known to this office was violently ransacked, presumably in a search for valuables which was not in vain, and one of the marauders thrust a cane through a priceless medieval painting portraying a biblical scene. . . . Jewish shop windows by the hundreds were systematically . . . smashed throughout the entire city. . . . Three synagogues in Leipzig were fired simultaneously by incendiary bombs and all sacred objects and records desecrated or destroyed, in most cases hurled through the windows and burned in the streets. No attempts whatsoever were made to quench the fires, the activity of the fire brigade being confined to playing water on adjoining buildings. All of the synagogues were irreparably gutted by flames.

non-Jews]. How often were we not told in the past that the removal of Jews from these institutions must lead to their collapse? . . . And what has actually happened? In all these spheres we are experiencing a vast flowering of cultural and artistic life.

Our films are better than ever before. The productions in our leading theatres stand in lonely preeminence over those of the whole world. Our Press has become a mighty instrument in the service of our people's self-preservation and contributes to strengthen the nation. German Science pursues its successful activity, while in architecture mighty evidences of our creative purpose will in the future bear witness to the achievements of this new age. There has been effected an unexampled immunization of the German people against all the disintegrating tendencies from which another world is forced to suffer.[49]

The führer's harsh, inhumane treatment of the Jews foreshadowed the manner in which he would deal with all of his enemies—including Poles, Slavs, French, British, and many others. In fact, he did not try to hide his sadistic intentions from close associates. "Do I intend to eradicate whole races?" he asked one of them. Answering his own question, he stated:

> Of course I do. . . . Cruelty is impressive. Cruelty and brutal strength. . . . The masses want it. They need the thrill of terror to make them shudderingly submissive. I do not want concentration camps to become old age pensioners' homes. Terror is the most effective way of politics.[50]

A Jewish synagogue burns during *Kristallnacht,* a wave of anti-Jewish terror.

An Aggressive Foreign Policy

As Hitler transformed Germany, often implementing policies he had first outlined in *Mein Kampf,* the rest of Europe began to worry about other ominous statements contained in the Nazi bible. Hitler had frankly discussed the inevitability of the *Anschluss,* the reunification of Germany and Austria; the need for German "living space" at the expense of the Russians and others; and the importance of getting revenge on France for the Versailles treaty and other past humiliations. Many Europeans nervously asked: Would the German dictator now implement such policies and threaten his neighbors?

Their answer was not long in coming. In 1934 Germany initiated a

The German army enters Czechoslovakia in March 1938. Allied leaders hoped this would be Hitler's last land grab, but they were wrong.

large-scale program of military rearmament and expansion in violation of the Versailles treaty, which had set limits on the size of its armed forces. And in 1936 Hitler and Italy's Fascist (right-wing dictatorial) leader, Benito Mussolini, signed a pact, creating the Berlin-Rome Axis. Some French, British, and American leaders recognized these events as the proverbial handwriting on the wall. British statesman Winston Churchill, for example, repeatedly warned that war with Germany and the Axis was inevitable if European politicians did not use diplomatic means to contain Hitler's ambitions. "Once Hitler's Germany had been allowed to rearm without active interference by the Allies," Churchill later wrote, a second World War was almost certain. The longer a decisive trial of strength was put off, the worse would be our chances, at first of stopping Hitler without serious fighting, and as a second stage of being victorious after a terrible ordeal. . . . Nazi Germany had secretly and unlawfully created a military air force which, by the spring of 1935, openly claimed to be equal to the British. . . . Great Britain and all Europe, and what was then thought distant America, were faced with the organized might and will-to-war of seventy millions of the most efficient race in Europe, longing to regain their national glory, and driven—in case they faltered—by a merciless

A Nazi Biology Text

*This is an excerpt from a German school text written in 1935—*Heredity and Racial Biology for Students, *by Joseph Graf (quoted in George Mosse's* Nazi Culture). *Subtitled "The Aryan: The Creative Force in Human History," the tract tells students that the superior "racial soul" of white, blond Aryans has dominated history and calls for critical examination of the "obviously inferior" traits of Jews. Excerpted here is the assignment section that students were asked to complete after reading the text.*

How We Can Learn to Recognize a Person's Race
ASSIGNMENTS
1. Summarize the spiritual characteristics of the individual races. . . .
5. Try to discover the intrinsic nature of the racial soul through the characters in stories and poetical works in terms of their inner attitude. Apply this mode of observation to persons in your own environment. . . .
9. Observe people whose special racial features have drawn your attention, also with respect to their bearing when moving or when speaking. Observe their expressions and gestures.
10. Observe the Jew: his way of walking, his bearing, gestures, and movements when talking. . . .
12. What are the occupations engaged in by the Jews of your acquaintance?
13. What are the occupations in which Jews are not to be found? Explain this phenomenon on the basis of the character of the Jew's soul.

military, social, and party regime. Hitler was now free to strike. . . . The Berlin-Rome Axis was in being. There was now, as it turned out, little hope of averting war or of postponing it by a trial of strength equivalent to war. Almost all that remained open to France and Britain was to await the moment of the challenge and do the best they could.[51]

Churchill's misgivings turned out to be well-founded, although none of his colleagues acted as decisively as he had hoped they would. Between 1935 and 1939, Allied leaders engaged in what later became known as a "policy of appeasement," in which they granted Hitler various concessions, in effect allowing him to get away with the seizure of neighboring lands. These aggressions included Austria and Czechoslovakia, which came under Nazi domination in 1938. In each case, the Allies hoped that Hitler would keep his promises and make no more territorial demands. Apparently they still did not grasp that he actually meant to carry out the foreboding, violent plans he had outlined in *Mein Kampf*.

Similarly, Soviet leader Joseph Stalin did not take seriously enough Hitler's anti-Russian rhetoric. Despite Hitler's earlier reference to the Soviets as the "scum of the earth" and Stalin's indictment of the Nazis as "bloody assassins of the workers," the two men stunned the world by signing a nonaggression pact in August 1939. According to historian Louis L. Snyder:

> The pact provided that the two parties would not resort to war against each other, would not support any third power in the event that it attacked either signatory, [and] would consult on all matters of common interest. . . . A secret protocol [clause] . . . divided eastern Europe into eventual German and Russian spheres, and each signatory was given territorial gains in the lands lying between them.[52]

Later Hitler would turn on the Russians in order to implement his diabolical blueprint for *Lebensraum*. For the moment, however, his cynical, cold-blooded bargain with Stalin provided the Nazis with the means of launching full-scale war. One of the "lands lying between" Germany and Russia became the first battleground of that war when Hitler attacked Poland on September 1, 1939.

Human Life Expendable

In a way, the war's outbreak marked the end of Germany's transition from an economically depressed, militarily weak, and pessimistic nation to an aggressive, militarily strong, and optimistic one. Unfortunately, any positive developments Hitler had brought about in the nation were thoroughly out-

Soviet leader Joseph Stalin (second from right) and other dignitaries watch as Russia's foreign minister signs a nonaggression pact with Germany in August 1939.

weighed by his brutal, repressive methods and deeds. And now, to further his own perverted agenda, he had committed the country to another world conflict in which thousands of German lives would have to be sacrificed.

To the führer, however, any loss of life, including that of Germans, was expendable, even inconsequential in his grand scheme of European conquest and domination. In his view, only his own life was truly important or in any way sacred. "No one will ever again have the confidence of the whole German people as I have," he told his generals in confidence. "There

will probably never again in the future be a man with more authority. My existence is, therefore, a factor of great value."[53] And to one of his doctors, he remarked, "I shall become the greatest man in history. I have to gain immortality even if the whole German nation perishes in the process."[54] Sadly for Germany, the individual who had uttered these astonishing words once more meant exactly what he said. Hitler had plunged humanity into the most devastating conflict it had ever known largely to satisfy the needs of his own monstrously misshapen ego.

Chapter Five

1939–1942: THE THIRD REICH AT ITS ZENITH

In a little less than twenty years, the Nazis had risen from obscurity to become a serious threat to global stability and human freedom. Within days following the German assault on Poland, most of the world's great powers had become locked in a titanic death struggle that would end up killing tens of millions of people and disrupting and forever changing the lives of hundreds of millions more. One by one, European countries rapidly fell to German steel, while German submarines attacked British and other Allied shipping in the Atlantic Ocean.

For the most part, Hitler's opponents had not been prepared for all-out war, especially against a military machine as formidable as the one the Nazis had assembled. Early in 1942, when the Third Reich was still at the zenith of its power and influence, as Louis Snyder explains,

> the *Wehrmacht* [German land forces] had between 260 and 300 divisions (25 armored or tank divisions, 35 motorized divisions, at least 200 infantry divisions, [and] from 4–8 airborne divisions), altogether between 7,000,000 and 10,000,000 troops. In the German Navy there were a half-dozen battleships, at least a dozen cruisers, two carriers, 30 to 40 destroyers, and from 125 to 175 submarines.

In the *Luftwaffe* [German air force] there were from five to seven air fleets with well over 5,000 tactical planes. And best of all from Hitler's viewpoint, these men were thoroughly trained, efficient, and in high morale.[55]

Maintaining these vast forces, as well as the German nation, during a major war was a tremendous logistical undertaking, to be sure. And Germany itself did not possess nearly enough oil, iron ore, food, and other vital raw materials to sustain such a mammoth effort for an extended period. Yet in Hitler's view, it did not need to. His plan was to loot and exploit the manpower, raw materials, and wealth of various other countries as he conquered them. At least at first, this plan seemed to work. In the first three to four years of the conflict, a gigantic mass of labor, raw materials, and money flowed into Nazi Germany, including workers from France, Belgium, and eastern Europe; oil from Romania; food from France, Denmark, and other lands; coal and grain from Poland; and iron ore from Scandinavia. Residents of Nazi occupied countries could do little or nothing to stop the loss of their young men, livestock, grain, farm and military equipment, fuel reserves, and other

More Demon than Human

Even as he ordered Germany's armies into battle, Hitler showed that he was not fully rational or in control of his own emotions and temper. The following recollection of one of his tantrums (quoted in Robert Waite's Psychopathic God) *is by a Swedish diplomat who visited Nazi headquarters in 1939.*

Hitler jumped up and became very agitated. He nervously paced up and down and declared, as if he were talking to himself, that Germany was invincible.... Suddenly he stopped in the middle of the room and stared straight ahead. His speech became more and more garbled, his whole behavior gave the impression of a person who was not at all himself. Sentences tumbled after one another...."If there is a war," he said, "I'll build U-Boats, U-Boats, U-Boats, U-Boats!" His voice became increasingly indistinct and gradually one could no longer understand him. Suddenly he collected himself, raised his voice as if addressing a vast assembly and screamed, "I'll build airplanes, airplanes, airplanes, airplanes and I'll annihilate my enemies!" At this moment he acted more like a demon in bad fiction than a human being. I looked at him in amazement.

precious resources as these things fed the growing, ever-voracious German colossus.

Adding to Hitler's strength and chances for success were his alliances with the other members of the Axis. Italy, led by its Fascist dictator Benito Mussolini, declared war on the Allies in June 1940; and Japan joined Germany and Italy in late September of the same year. The three countries signed a ten-year alliance known as the Tripartite Pact, pledging to support one another both militarily and economically. By May 1941 Nazi Germany and the Axis dominated almost all the nations in non-Soviet Europe. Himmler's SS and Gestapo moved into these territories to impose terror and order and thereby reduce the chance of any resistance or uprisings. At the height of his power, Hitler also began the systematic mass murder of those Europeans he deemed inferior, including the Jews.

Britain and France Declare War

To a large extent, the boldness of Germany's aggressive moves in the war's first three years was inspired by Hitler's overwhelming, and as it turned out irrational, confidence. He was absolutely convinced that he was a godlike savior and brilliant strategist, while most or all of his opponents were weak, stupid, cowardly, subhuman, or all of these. Still, the fear of an untime-

ly death and his having too little time to complete his goals plagued him; so he insisted that German conquests proceed quickly, whether or not his advisers thought it prudent. On the eve of invading Poland, for example, he told his generals:

> Our enemies have men who are below average, no personalities, no masters, no men of action. . . . For us it is easy to make decisions. We have nothing to lose; we have everything to gain. . . . All these favorable circumstances will no longer prevail in two or three years. . . . Therefore conflict is better now. I am afraid that at the last minute some Schweinehund [pig-dog] will make a proposal for mediation. . . . I shall give a propagandist reason for starting the war, no matter whether it is plausible or not. The victor will not be asked, later on, whether he told the truth or not. In starting and waging war, it is not the Right that matters, but Victory.[56]

Because he saw British and French leaders as weaklings, Hitler expected them to do little or nothing, outside of verbal condemnations, in response to his invasion of Poland, which began on September 1, 1939. So he was duly surprised when both of these nations entered the war against Germany on September 3. That day British prime minister Neville Chamberlain sadly issued the following message to his people:

This morning the British ambassador in Berlin handed to the German government a final note that unless we heard from them by 11 o'clock that they were prepared at once to withdraw their troops from Poland, a state of war would exist between us. I have to tell you now that no such undertaking has been received and that consequently this country is at war with Germany. . . . Now may God bless you all and may He defend the right. For it is evil things that we shall be fighting against—brute force, bad faith, injustice, oppression, and persecution. And against them I am certain that the right will prevail.[57]

The Collapse of France

Though angry at Britain's and France's entry into the war, Hitler was not overly worried. Sooner or later, he reasoned, he would have had to fight them; so why not do so sooner? In any case, his nonaggression pact with

German Advances, 1939–1940

Northern Ireland

NORTH SEA

NORWAY

SWEDEN

BALTIC

ESTONIA
SOVIET OCCUPIED

SOVIET OCCUPIED

Germany invades Denmark and Norway April 1940

UNITED KINGDOM

DENMARK

SEA

LATVIA

IRELAND

LITHUANIA

Germany invades Low Countries May 1940

GREAT BRITAIN

Danzig

ATLANTIC OCEAN

London

NETHERLANDS

Berlin

EAST PRUSSIA

Soviet Occupied

Battle of France May–June 1940

Dunkerque

BELGIUM

GERMANY

Lodz

Warsaw

POLAND

Paris

LUX.

WWII begins when Germany invades Poland September 1, 1939

SLOVAKIA

Germany, Austria, and Slovakia

Allied Nations

Neutral Nations

German Occupation

Soviet Occupation

German Drives

Vichy

SWITZ.

AUSTRIA

HUNGARY

FRANCE

ITALY

ROMANIA

Danube R.

YUGOSLAVIA

Stalin left his eastern flank safe for the moment, allowing him to concentrate on crushing his opponents in the west. This he did, in most cases with brutal efficiency. In the first months of 1940, German troops occupied Denmark and Norway and overwhelmed Belgium, Holland, and Luxembourg.

It now became obvious that France would be the führer's next target. On June 5, 1940, some 143 German armored divisions swept into northeastern France and pushed the much weaker French forces backward. No match for the Germans, these native forces soon melted away, and Hitler's troops entered an undefended Paris on June 14. Almost immediately, Nazi henchmen planted a swastika on the Eiffel Tower as undetermined numbers of helpless French watched in despair or wept. Though swift, the invasion had not been bloodless, especially for the losers. In fewer than two weeks, the French and their allies had suffered 90,000 dead, 200,000 injured, and 1.9 million captured or missing; while only 30,000 Germans had been killed.

On hearing the news of France's fall, Hitler was ecstatic. One of his most impassioned goals—the humbling of the nation that had most humiliated Germany at the close of the Great War—was finally fulfilled. In a symbolic gesture of revenge, the führer chose to hold the surrender ceremony on the very spot where Germany had capitulated to the

Allies in 1918. Journalist William Shirer was there, on the edge of the forest at Compiègne (northeast of Paris) on June 21 when Hitler and his chief cronies arrived. "I observed his face," Shirer recorded.

Hitler tours Paris in June 1940 after Germany's defeat of France.

Churchill Defies Hitler

Hitler's villainy and the threat he posed to free nations everywhere was not lost on Allied leaders like Winston Churchill. As the rescue ships from Dunkerque were unloading in southern England, the British leader issued this speech of defiance (quoted from The War Speeches of Churchill*), which remains one of the most inspiring in modern annals.*

Even though large tracts of Europe and many old and famous States have fallen or may fall into the grip of the Gestapo and all the odious apparatus of Nazi rule, we shall not flag or fail. We shall go on to the end, we shall fight in France, we shall fight in the seas and oceans, we shall fight with growing confidence and growing strength in the air, we shall defend our island, whatever the cost may be, we shall fight on the beaches, we shall fight on the landing grounds, we shall fight in the fields and in the streets, we shall fight in the hills; we shall never surrender, and even if, which I do not for a moment believe, this island or a large part of it were subjugated and starving, then our Empire beyond the seas, armed and guarded by the British Fleet, would carry on the struggle, until, in God's good time, the New World [i.e., the United States], with all its power and might, steps forth to the rescue and the liberation of the Old.

Britain's prime minister, Winston Churchill, gave the Allies hope.

It was grave, solemn, yet brimming with revenge. There was also in it, as in his springy step, a note of the triumphant conqueror, the defier of the world. There was something else . . . a sort of scornful, inner joy at being present at this great reversal of fate—a reversal he himself had wrought.[58]

That night, after speaking to Hitler by phone from Berlin, Goebbels remarked,

"The disgrace is now extinguished. It's a feeling of being born again."[59]

Confrontation with Britain

Hitler's victory over France seemed all the more sweet to him because he himself had planned most of its major strategy. (It should be noted that this was one of only a few instances in the war in which one of his own battle plans was successful.) He had made one serious error, however. Namely, he had failed to cut off the escape route for large numbers of British and Belgian troops who had been aiding the French. Between May 26 and June 14, 1940, some 338,000 British, Belgian, and French troops retreated to Dunkerque, in extreme northern France. From there a ragtag flotilla of nearly nine hundred vessels—of every conceivable type, large and small—evacuated them across the English Channel to safety while the Royal Air Force (RAF) held German bombers at bay.

The arrogant Hitler merely shrugged off the so-called "miracle" of Dunkerque. He still held out hope that "cowardly" Britain would be too afraid to continue fighting and soon sue for peace. He was dead wrong, however. The British, now led by a new, highly capable prime minister, Winston Churchill, remained defiant. Surprised once more and intent on teaching Britain a lesson, Hitler unleashed the Luftwaffe, which launched all-out attacks on British ports, industrial sites,

and eventually London. The goal was to cripple the country in preparation for an invasion, to be called Operation Sea Lion. But said invasion never occurred. The outnumbered RAF fought back in a desperate, heroic effort that came to be known as the Battle of Britain; after losing more than seventeen hundred planes, Hitler decided to postpone Operation Sea Lion and deal with Britain later. Churchill expressed the thanks of a grateful nation when he said of the brave band of British airmen: "Undaunted by odds, unwearied in their constant challenge and mortal danger, [they turned] the tide of the World War by their prowess and their devotion. Never in the field of human conflict was so much owed by so many to so few."[60]

Russia Betrayed

In Hitler's view, despite the success of the RAF, his bombing of Britain had left that land devastated and nearly defenseless. Believing that for the moment the British did not constitute a credible threat, he suddenly turned his attention to the east. In late 1940 and early 1941, he rapidly managed to bring the Balkan countries, including Romania with its valuable oil supplies, under Axis control.

Finally, the führer felt he held enough of a favorable strategic and logistical position to turn on and attack the Soviets. He had always seen his pact with Stalin as a temporary mea-

Berlin Bombed for the First Time

On August 23, 1940, during bombing runs over Britain, German planes struck the heart of London, killing a number of civilians. In retaliation, the next night British pilots bombed Berlin, as described by American journalist William L. Shirer, in this excerpt from his massive Rise and Fall of the Third Reich.

It didn't amount to much. There was a dense cloud cover over Berlin that night and only about half of the eighty-one RAF bombers dispatched found the target. Material damage was negligible. But the effect on German morale was tremendous. *For this was the first time that bombs had ever fallen on Berlin.* "The Berliners are stunned," I wrote in my diary the next day, August 26. "They did not think it could ever happen. When this war began, [Nazi leader Hermann] Goering assured them it couldn't.... They believed him. Their disillusionment today therefore is all the greater. You have to see their faces to measure it." Berlin was well defended by two great rings of antiaircraft and for three hours while the visiting bombers droned above the clouds, which prevented the hundreds of searchlight batteries from picking them up, the flak fire was the most intense I had ever seen. But not a single plane was brought down. The British also dropped a few leaflets saying that "the war which Hitler started will go on, and it will last as long as Hitler does." This was good propaganda, but the thud of exploding bombs was better.

sure designed to allow him the freedom he needed to conquer France and other parts of western Europe. Now that that goal had been achieved, he could implement the diabolical scheme he had long ago outlined in *Mein Kampf*—to seek "living space" for his master race at the expense of the Slavs. Accordingly, on June 22, 1941, the Nazis launched Operation Barbarossa, invading Russia with 121 divisions. Because the Russians were taken completely by surprise, German forces made incredibly quick headway, advancing more than four hundred miles in only eighteen days. And by the end of July, more than a million Soviet soldiers had been captured.

As usual, Hitler was confident of total victory. Expecting that Soviet Russia would collapse relatively swiftly, he issued orders to his generals to show no mercy to the Russian cities, which were to be annihilated. "A capitulation of Leningrad or Moscow is not to be accepted, even if offered,"[61] he declared on September 18. Another order, dated September 29, read:

The Führer has decided to have St. Petersburg [Leningrad] wiped off the face of the earth. The further existence of this large city is of no interest once Soviet Russia is overthrown. . . . The intention is to close in on the city and raze it to the ground by artillery and by continuous air attack. . . . Requests that the city be taken over will be turned down, for *the problem of the survival of the population, and of supplying it with food is one which cannot and should not be solved by us.* In this war for existence we have no interest in keeping [alive] even part of this great city's population [emphases in the original].[62]

The evil plans Hitler had for the Russians and other eastern Slavs once Russia had been defeated are clear, not only from Hitler's own earlier writings, but also from various surviving remarks by leading Nazis during the war. Himmler, who had already begun mapping out an SS campaign to brutalize and exploit the Slavic survivors, showed a callous indifference to what were

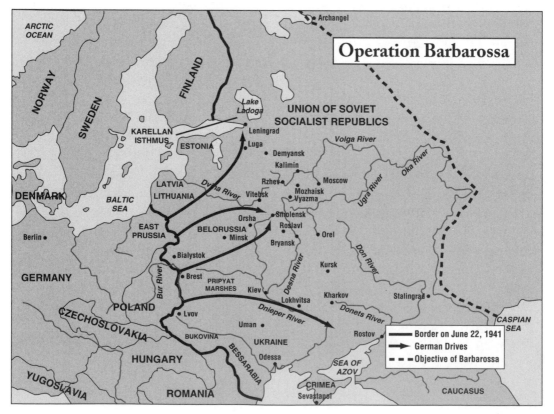

nothing less than crimes against humanity. "What happens to a Russian, to a Czech, does not interest me in the slightest," he told his SS chiefs.

What the [conquered] nations can offer in the way of good blood of our type, we will take, if necessary by kidnapping their children and raising them here with us. Whether nations live in prosperity or starve to death like cattle interests me only in so far as we need them as slaves to our [culture]; otherwise it is of no interest to me. Whether 10,000 Russian females fall down from exhaustion while digging an antitank ditch interests me only in so far as the antitank ditch for Germany is finished.[63]

Another leading Nazi, Erich Koch, the Reich commander in the Ukraine, said in a speech delivered at Kiev:

We are the Master Race and must govern hard. . . . I did not come [to Russia] to spread bliss. . . . The population must work, work, and work again. . . . We are a master race, which must remember that the lowliest German worker is racially and biologically a thousand times more valuable than [any member of] the population here.[64]

Hitler agreed, saying in July 1941:

As for the ridiculous hundred million Slavs, we will mold the best of them to the shape that suits us, and we will isolate the rest of them in their own pigsties; and anyone who talks about cherishing the local inhabitant and civilizing him, goes straight off to a concentration camp![65]

The Holocaust Begins

Hitler, Himmler, and the other Nazi leaders employed similar cruel and racist rhetoric against the Jews, whom they hated even more than the Slavs and Poles. There is not the slightest doubt that Hitler intended to eradicate the Jews, certainly those in Germany and preferably in all of Europe, once he had secured most of the continent. On five separate occasions before the conflict had even begun, he had spelled it out with brutal clarity in public speeches, though not many people at the time took these threats seriously. "If the international Jewish financiers . . . should again succeed in plunging the nations into a world war," he warned in the Reichstag in January 1939, "the result will be . . . the annihilation of the Jewish race throughout Europe."[66] As Shirer has pointed out:

It made no difference that not the "international Jewish financiers" but he himself plunged the world into armed conflict. What mattered

A Nazi SS killing squad murders a group of defenseless Russian civilians, whose bodies fill one of hundreds of mass graves created by Hitler's henchmen.

to Hitler was that there was now a world war and that it afforded him, after he had conquered vast regions in the East where most of Europe's Jews lived, the opportunity to carry out their "annihilation." By the time the invasion of Russia began, he had given the necessary orders.[67]

At a later date, Himmler alluded to those orders when he spoke to his SS generals about the so-called "Final Solution" to the Jewish "problem." Fearful of the judgment of history, as was the führer himself, Himmler cautioned them about the importance of secrecy. "We will never speak of it publicly," he said. "I mean . . . the extermination of the Jewish race. . . . This is a page of glory in our history which has never been written and is never to be written."[68]

The Final Solution was in many ways simply a larger-scale continuation of mass-murder policies Hitler already had in place. Since the late 1930s, he had been killing thousands of handicapped and mentally ill persons each year. And after invading Russia, mobile SS killing squads—the *Einsatzgruppen*—had roamed the country-side, slaughtering large numbers of political leaders, Communists, Gypsies, and Jews. (The largest single mass killing in this cam-paign occurred at Babi Yar, near Kiev, where some thirty-three thousand people died.)

At first, most European Jews were rounded up and forced to live in ghet-tos, usually urban areas sectioned off by brick walls or barbed wire. But by the middle of 1941, the Holocaust (the sys-tematic mass murder of the Jews) had begun. SS guards herded Jews from the ghettos like cattle into overcrowded train cars and shipped them to various death camps scattered around central Europe. At the height of the program, about thirty such camps existed.

It quickly became clear that killing large numbers of people was time-consuming; so those in charge of the operation searched for the most effi-cient methods they could find. One of the commanders of the infamous camp at Auschwitz, Rudolf Höss, later recalled:

I was ordered to establish extermi-nation facilities at Auschwitz in

Ukranian Jewish women and children are stripped and herded together. Minutes after this photo was taken, Nazi soldiers shot them in cold blood.

A gas chamber at the infamous death camp at Auschwitz (top); and ovens for incinerating bodies at the camp at Weimar (right). Millions of Jews met their ends in such facilities.

June 1941. At that time there were already in the General Government of Poland three other extermination camps: Belzec, Treblinka and Wolzek. . . . I visited Treblinka to find out how they carried out their extermination. The camp commandant at Treblinka told me that he had liquidated 80,000 in the course of half a year. He was principally concerned with liquidating all the Jews from the

Warsaw ghetto. He used monoxide gas and I did not think that his methods were very efficient. So when I set up the extermination building at Auschwitz, I used Zyklon B, which was a crystallized prussic acid which we dropped into the death chamber from a small opening. It took from three to fifteen minutes to kill the people in the death chamber, depending upon climatic conditions. We knew when the people were dead because their screaming stopped. We usually waited about a half hour before we opened the doors and removed the bodies. After the bodies were removed, our special commandos took off the rings and extracted the gold from the teeth of the corpses. Another improvement we [at Auschwitz] made over Treblinka was that we built our gas chambers to accommodate 2,000 people at one time, whereas at Treblinka their ten gas chambers only accommodated 200 people each.[69]

Using these gruesome methods, the killing became highly efficient indeed. Auschwitz alone was eventually able to exterminate up to six thousand people a day.

Once these atrocities were in motion on a large scale, Hitler felt vindicated for all the times in the past when people had taken his ideas and threats concerning the Jews lightly. In a public speech given in 1942, in which he bragged of the recent successes of the Third Reich, then at its zenith, he mentioned how people had once scoffed at his prediction that the Jews would be annihilated. "People always laughed at me as a prophet," he said. "Of those who laughed then," he added in a chilling tone of voice, "innumerable numbers no longer laugh today."[70]

Chapter Six

1943–1945: Death of a Twisted Dream

Though Hitler's Reich enjoyed a period of success in the early years of the war, ultimately the Nazi regime and its totalitarian ambitions were doomed to failure. As time went on, a number of factors increasingly hampered Germany's war effort. The Allies hammered at "fortress Europe" on numerous fronts, spreading thin and draining German resources; Allied bombing of German cities destroyed both materials and morale; and the German military made too many costly mistakes. The latter were mostly the fault of Hitler himself, who insisted on making important decisions in areas in which he was not qualified. Nazi architect Albert Speer, who served as minister of armaments during the war, remembered:

From the start of my work . . . I discovered blunder after blunder, in all departments of the economy. Incongruously enough, Hitler himself used to say during those war years: "The loser of this war will be the side that makes the greatest blunders." For Hitler, by a succession of wrong-headed decisions, helped to speed the end of a war already lost because of [insufficient] productive capacities—for example, by his confused planning of the air war against England, by the shortage of U-boats [submarines] at the beginning of the war, and, in general, by his failure to develop an overall plan for the war. So that when many German memoirs comment on Hitler's decisive mistakes, the writers are completely right.[71]

One of the most telling of the führer's "wrong-headed decisions" was his insistence on wasting precious German time, resources, and manpower on capturing, transporting, and exterminating Jews. Robert Waite describes the military consequences of this policy:

Hitler's personal phobia about Jews contributed to Germany's military defeat. As Albert Speer

In this photo taken on May 5, 1943, Hitler confers with Nazi Armaments Minister Albert Speer on the strength of German defenses along the Atlantic coast.

has reported, a key reason why Germany never attempted to develop the atomic bomb was that the Führer distrusted what he called "Jewish physics." And his personal orders to kill all the Jews in Europe resulted in serious disruptions of the national war effort. The sheer logistics of collecting, transporting, and disposing of so many [people] . . . were immense. . . . By 1944, the shortage of labor created by removing Jews from the work force ran to some 4 million men; the value in war production lost to the Reich amounted to billions of Reichsmarks. Viewed pragmatically [practically], genocide was counterproductive. During the militarily disastrous years of

80

Attempts to Demoralize the Enemy

As the Allied armies advanced on Germany, the Germans dropped leaflets designed to demoralize or frighten the Allied soldiers, as in this example (quoted in Louis Snyder's The War).

YOUR FIRST WINTER IN EUROPE. EASY GOING HAS STOPPED!

Perhaps you've already noticed it—the nearer the German border, the heavier your losses. Naturally. They're defending their own homes. Winter is just around the corner—hence diminishing A.F. [air force] activity. More burden on the shoulders of the infantry, therefore heavier casualties. WHO IS CASHING IN ON THE HUGE WAR PROFITS AT HOME, WHILE AMERICANS SHED THEIR BLOOD OVER HERE [a reference to American Jewish businessmen]?

1943–1945, Germany simply could not afford to embark on the "final solution" to a problem which never in fact existed.[72]

As a result of these and other factors, the Nazi war machine sputtered and the Allies slowly but steadily began to close in on the German heartland. Especially telling was the increasing role played by the United States. In the conflict's early years, Hitler had underestimated the potential power of the Americans. By contrast, Churchill had fully realized that, once committed to the fighting, the United States would prove to be a virtually unstoppable force. Sooner or later, he declared, this force would turn the tide in the battle against the Axis nations. Churchill later wrote:

No American will think it wrong of me if I proclaim that to have the United States at our side was to me the greatest joy. . . . Hitler's fate was sealed. . . . [Italy's] fate was sealed. As for the Japanese, they would be ground to powder. All the rest was merely the proper application of overwhelming force.[73]

Allied Advances, German Retreats

One of Hitler's most serious mistakes was to underestimate Russia's determination and resources. He expected Soviet resistance to collapse quickly; after all, he thought, mere Slavs could never get the better of his superior Aryan troops. Once again, the führer was allowing his sick ideology to cloud reality and good judgment. By the end of 1941, the Russians had begun to regroup; and in the next two years, they staged increasing counteroffensives. These drove the Germans back from Leningrad and Moscow. Meanwhile, Hitler refused to permit his forces to retreat from Stalingrad; more than 300,000 Germans were killed, and in February 1943 100,000 more surrendered to the Russians.

Meanwhile, Hitler's forces encountered increasing problems all over Europe. German losses in the Battle of Britain and the debacle at Stalingrad showed the peoples of Europe that the Nazis were not invincible, spurring underground resistance groups in the occupied countries to become bolder and better organized; aided by British and American intelligence agents, they assassinated Nazi officials, blew up trains and factories, and helped escaped prisoners of war.

The British and Americans also staged daring bombing raids on German cities. In the summer of 1943, for example, a raid destroyed three-quarters of the city of Hamburg. In his diary, Joseph Goebbels described some of the devastation:

July 26. During the night a heavy raid on Hamburg . . . with most serious consequences both for the civilian population and for armaments production. . . . It is a real catastro-

phe. . . . July 29. During the night we had the heaviest raid yet made on Hamburg . . . with 800 to 1,000 [Allied] bombers . . . a catastrophe the extent of which simply staggers the imagination. A city of a million inhabitants has been destroyed in a manner unparalleled in history. We are faced with problems that are almost impossible of solution. Food must be found for this population. . . . Shelter must be secured. The people must be evacuated as far [away from further danger] as possible. . . . Some 800,000 homeless people . . . are wandering up and down the streets not knowing what to do.[74]

Goebbels's concern for German civilians was not shared by his boss. The propaganda chief could not understand why the führer consistently refused to visit Hamburg, or any other bombed-out city for that matter, to comfort and give hope to the people. Even a hardened Nazi like Goebbels was unable to grasp how little Hitler cared for human life, much less people's feelings and needs. Goebbels could only watch with mounting distress as Allied bombing attacks continued month after month, culminating in one that ignited an enormous firestorm in Dresden on February 13, 1945, and killed at least sixty thousand people.

At the same time, the Allies increasingly went on the offensive. In July 1943 British and American forces

American troops disembark from their landing craft during the D day invasion at Normandy, in June 1944. The noose had begun to close on Hitler's Germany.

landed in Sicily. Not long afterward, on July 25, Mussolini was suddenly overthrown; fearing the Italians would sue for peace, Nazi forces took control of Italy's strategic centers and awaited the Allied assault. That attack began in September, and by June 4, 1944, Rome was under Allied control. Just two days later, on what became known as D day, the Allies began their enormous assault on the beaches of Normandy (in northwestern France); within three

Hitler shows Italian dictator Benito Mussolini the remains of the Nazi leader's headquarters following the failed assasination attempt by Claus von Stauffenberg.

weeks, more than a million American, British, and other Allied soldiers had begun to sweep eastward across France and toward the German border.

The Plot to Kill Hitler

With the Allies approaching from the west and south and the Russians from the east, Germany was caught in a deadly vise. Many German generals had long before this recognized that their cause was hopeless, and the new enemy onslaught only reinforced this conclusion. But Hitler refused to consider any notions of defeat or surrender; it would be better if every man,

woman, and child in Germany died, he told some of his associates. Fed up with the führer's fatalistic attitude, a group of his officers decided to take matters into their own hands. They were led by Colonel Claus S. von Stauffenberg. As Louis Snyder memorably puts it:

> He came to the conclusion that Hitler's lunatic disregard for human decency had so besmirched the name of the German fatherland that it stank in the nostrils of civilized men everywhere. He would assassinate this madman and bring an end to the senseless war.[75]

On July 20, 1944, von Stauffenberg placed a bomb in a briefcase and carried it into a command post in northern Germany where Hitler was meeting with some of his top military officers. The would-be assassin placed the case near Hitler's feet, excused himself, and walked out; but seconds later another officer, feeling the case was in his way, moved it to the outside of one of the heavy table supports. At 12:42 P.M. the bomb exploded, destroying the command post; four men died instantly, but the table support protected the führer from the full force of the blast; his legs were burned, his right arm injured, and his right ear permanently deafened, but he was very much alive.

The conspirators made other mistakes as well, and the attempted coup failed. Furious, Hitler went on the radio to assure the German people that reports of his death were premature. "I was spared a fate which held no horror for me," he said, "but would have had terrible consequences for the German people. I see in it a sign from Providence that I must, and therefore shall, continue

Astrology Predicts a Nazi Victory?

In the last days of the war, as Germany was collapsing around him, the desperate and demented Hitler fell back on, among other things, mysticism and astrology, which he believed predicted his ultimate victory. In these statements (quoted in Chester Wilmot's Struggle for Europe*), Nazi propaganda chief Joseph Goebbels summed up the supposedly favorable prophecies of two horoscopes, one cast in 1918, the other in 1933.*

An amazing fact has become evident, both horoscopes predicting the outbreak of the war in 1939, the victories until 1941, and the subsequent series of reversals, with the hardest blows during the first months of 1945, particularly during the first half of April. In the second half of April we were to experience a temporary success. Then there would be stagnation until August and peace that same month. For the following three years Germany would have a hard time, but starting in 1948 she would rise again. . . . The Führer has declared that even in this very year a change of fortune shall come. . . . The true quality of genius is its consciousness and its sure knowledge of coming change. The Führer knows the exact hour of its arrival. Destiny has sent us this man so that we, in this time of great external and internal stress, shall testify to the miracle [of the Nazis' deliverance].

Grim-faced, Hitler, accompanied by top Nazi officers, surveys the destruction of a German city caused by Allied bombing in 1944.

my work."[76] The plotters were captured and felt the full fury of Hitler's wrath. He ordered almost all members of the von Stauffenberg family killed and had the plot's eight ringleaders hanged from meat hooks in such a way that they took up to five minutes to die from strangulation. He also ordered a film crew to record the brutal spectacle and later gleefully watched the film over and over.

The War No Longer Winnable

The execution of the conspirators may have made Hitler feel better about himself and the war effort. But most of his generals were fast reaching the same conclusion von Stauffenberg had—that the war was no longer winnable. On August 25, 1944, the Americans liberated Paris; and a few days later, the Russians captured Romania, depriving the Reich of its only major source of oil. Meanwhile, German armies were in full retreat on most fronts. By the end of August, Germany's western forces alone had lost more than 500,000 men (about half of them as prisoners) and nearly all of their tanks and trucks. "As far as I was concerned," Field Marshal Gerd von Rundstedt later recalled, "the war was ended in September [1944]."[77]

But the führer insisted on fighting on, no matter what the consequences. "If necessary we'll fight on the Rhine," he said.

> It doesn't make any difference. Under all circumstances we will continue this battle until . . . one of our damned enemies gets too tired to fight anymore. We'll fight until we get a peace which secures the life of the German nation for the next fifty or a hundred years and which, above all, does not besmirch our honor a second time, as happened in 1918. . . . I live only for the purpose of leading this fight because I know that if there is not an iron will behind it, this battle cannot be won.[78]

Believing in the fantasy that the Allies would suddenly begin fighting each other and forget about attacking Germany, the unbalanced Hitler instructed von Rundstedt to launch one more mighty offensive in the west. That assault, which began in December 1944, resulted in the bloody confrontation known as the Battle of the Bulge. Despite considerable bravery shown by the German forces, they could not stem the Allied tide. In January 1945, having sustained another 120,000 casualties, the Germans withdrew, allowing the Allied advance to continue.

After that, the end came quickly for Adolf Hitler and his Third Reich. By April 27, 1945, the Russians had completely surrounded Berlin with an awesome array of military might. It included some 2.5 million well-armed and battle-hardened troops, 42,000 artillery pieces, 6,250 tanks, and 7,560 warplanes. To meet this juggernaut, Hitler had only 44,000 soldiers and another 45,000 old men and young boys, every two of whom had to share a rifle.

Faced with total defeat, Hitler, true to form, became hysterical and blamed others for his own mistakes. General Heinz Guderian later remembered witnessing a two-hour-long temper tantrum:

His fists raised, his cheeks flushed with rage, his whole body trembling, the man stood there in front of me, beside himself with fury and having lost all self-control. After each outburst Hitler would stride up and down the carpet edge, then suddenly stop immediately before me and hurl his next accusation in my face. He was almost screaming,

The Mystery of Hitler's Lake

This is part of the transcript of the July 25, 2001, broadcast of the television newsmagazine 60 Minutes II, *describing the recent discovery of evidence for what was perhaps Hitler's last nefarious scheme against the Allies.*

Imagine a lake more mysterious than Loch Ness—a lake that hides a secret no one was meant to discover. There is such a place high up in the Austrian Alps. It is a lake called Toplitz. Early one morning in 1945, Nazi SS officers sank a number of wooden boxes in Toplitz.... Last summer, *60 Minutes II* led an underwater expedition in search of those boxes.... Its crew found evidence of a Nazi plot you didn't read about in your history books.

What's in Hitler's lake? ... Feb. 23, 1945: Hitler's Reich was tumbling down. The Allies were closing in and, in bombed-out Berlin, the Nazis were scrambling to truck their most valuable secrets out of town. Adolf Burger was expecting to die at the Sachsenhausen concentration camp. He was the man who knew too much—a Jew who had been forced to work on a top-secret Nazi plot.... He and several other prisoners were forced to participate in a covert Nazi project: creating fake currency to crash Allied economies—including that of the United States....

The project was part of a Nazi scheme to print money on a vast scale (the equivalent of $4.5 billion), most of it in British pounds. ... It was Hitler's secret weapon. The idea was to flood the world with bogus money to undermine the Allied currencies and, at the same time, help pay for the war.... According to Burger, "The first 200 bills were finished on Feb. 22, 1945. We were supposed to start printing the first million dollars the next day. But on that day, Feb. 23, there was an order ... to stop work and dismantle the machinery. The Russians were 300 kilometers from Berlin." ... When the project was abruptly ended, Burger was told to pack the counterfeit currency into boxes. He didn't know at the time, but ... the Nazis planned to evacuate Hitler and a guerrilla army to the region around Lake Toplitz.

The body claimed by some to be that of Hitler after his suicide in late April 1945. The authenticity of the photo has been disputed.

his eyes seemed to pop out of his head and the veins stood out in his temples.[79]

There were many other such outbursts. His generals and soldiers were cowards, Hitler charged, and everyone he had trusted had betrayed him. On hearing that Himmler had, on his own initiative, begun secret peace negotiations with the Western Allies, the führer whined: "Nothing now remains! Nothing is spared me! No loyalty is kept, no honor observed! There is no bitterness, no betrayal that has not yet been heaped upon me!"[80]

The Coward's Way Out

Hitler's death and that of his twisted dream of world conquest came on April 30, 1945, in a concrete bunker deep beneath the streets of Berlin. The day before, he had married his longtime mistress, Eva Braun. (He had met her in 1929, when she was seventeen and working in the office of his photographer. Over the years he had kept her more or less closeted away from public view in one or another of his apartments. Though he often humiliated her in front of his associates and she attempted suicide several times, she loved him and remained loyal to the end.) After lunch on the thirtieth, the führer had his favorite dog, Blondi, shot; then he and his new bride retired to his suite.

The exact details of the couple's suicides and cremation remain uncertain, and numerous theories have been advanced to explain them. The best guess is that at about 3:30 that afternoon, Hitler swallowed a lethal dose of cyanide, after which Eva shot him in the left temple with a revolver. Then she took the same poison, curled up beside him, and expired. Some subordinates carried the bodies up to the chancellery courtyard, soaked them in gasoline, and set them ablaze. The corpses burned for at least two hours; but they were not totally destroyed, since Russian agents soon found the remains and positively identified them.

Among the last press releases by Nazi officials was one stating that Hitler had died a "heroic death," fighting against the invaders with his last breath. He had fallen "at the head of the heroic defenders of the Reich capital."[81] Only later did the Germans learn the truth: Befitting the disreputable character he had always displayed, the creator of the obscenity known as Nazism had taken the coward's way out and left his followers to face the world's wrath.

Monument to a Monster

Nothing could ever compensate for the mass death and misery Hitler and his Nazis had caused. But at least there was a small touch of poetic justice. In his final moments in that dismal underground bunker, as the Allied shells roared and pounded above him, the realization of a terrible truth must have filled him with rage and regret. The glorious Reich he had vowed would last for a thousand years had rather pathetically missed the mark by 988 years.

During the Reich's tumultuous twelve years of existence, Hitler had promised to elevate Germany to eternal glory; but the Nazi reign had instead brought the nation and much of the rest of Europe untold devastation and misery. Berlin and other German cities lay in ruins and some 7 million German soldiers and civilians lay dead. Almost 6 million Jews had been exterminated in Nazi death camps during the war. And added to these gruesome figures were those of other European and Allied deaths, bringing the overall toll in Europe to a staggering 40 million.

Clearly, the ordeal of total war that Europe and the world had endured between 1939 and 1945 had been the largest single conflict, with the most far-reaching consequences, of any in history. In large degree, the war had been Hitler's creation. The twisted dreams of one man had ended up shattering those of millions of people and forever transforming the borders, goals, and fortunes of dozens of nations. In John Toland's words:

Adolph Hitler was probably the greatest mover and shaker of the twentieth century. Certainly no other human disrupted so many lives in our times or stirred so much hatred. He also inspired widespread adoration and was the hope and ideal of millions. . . . To the few who remained his faithful followers he is a hero, a fallen Messiah; to the rest he is still a madman, a political and military bungler, an evil murderer beyond redemption whose successes were reached by criminal means.[82]

Emergence of a New Germany

The legacy of history's most infamous villain began when German envoys

Nazis on trial at Nuremburg following the close of the war. The first three men in the front row (from left to right) are Hermann Göering, Rudolph Hess, and Joachim von Ribbentrop.

surrendered unconditionally to the Allies on May 7, 1945. The führer's devastated, humiliated country now faced further depredations. From November 1945 to October 1946, surviving Nazi Party leaders and high German officials went on trial at Nuremberg, the site of so many huge Nazi rallies. An international panel of judges sentenced twelve men to death, three to life in prison, and four to shorter prison terms. (Albert Speer received a sentence of twenty years; three others were acquitted.)

In addition, the Allies divided both Berlin and Germany into four zones (the American, French, British, and Soviet); in 1949 the Western Allies consolidated their areas into the Federal Republic of Germany (or West Germany), while the Soviet zone became the Communist-run German Democratic Republic (or East Germany). In the forty years that followed (until the Berlin Wall, a barrier erected by the Communists in 1961, came down in 1990), the Germans remained divided. Those in East Germany continued to suffer as the Nazi dictatorship was replaced by a Communist one.

Eventually, with the help of the Western nations, especially the United States, the Germans rebuilt their wartorn country. And today West and East Germany are united once more as one of the leading European nations and a strong democracy. The Germans finally learned the value of democratic ideals, in large part because of Hitler's extremism. "In its maelstrom [storm] of destruction," Ian Kernshaw points out, "Hitler's rule had . . . conclusively demonstrated the utter bankruptcy of the hyper-nationalistic and racist world power ambitions . . . that had prevailed in Germany [before]. . . . The old Germany was gone with Hitler."[83]

The Cancer of Collective Guilt

Yet the shame of what Germany, led by Hitler and his Nazis, had done to Europe and the world remained. To this day the Germans remain imprinted by the moral stain of Nazi conquests and haunted by the ghosts of the Holocaust. In May 1945 an anonymous resident of Munich painted on a wall, "I am ashamed to be a German."[84] With the passage of decades and the rise of new generations that did not remember life under the Nazis, this sad sentiment has in large degree faded from German life and consciousness; yet the collective guilt remains in the culture's *sub*conscious, lurking like an unwanted, incurable cancer. "The Germans have been liberated from Hitler, yet they will never be free of him," German historian Eberhard Jäckel writes.

He himself will never return, and even the danger of another monarchy like his is remote in view of current social developments. . . .

But it is important to note that even the dead Hitler will always remain with the Germans, with the survivors, with their descendants, and even with the unborn. He will be with them, not as he was with his contemporaries, but as an eternal monument to what is humanly possible.[85]

Ironically, that monument to a monster may well last the thousand years that his Reich did not.

NOTES

Introduction: Memory of a False Messiah

1. William L. Shirer, *Berlin Diary: The Journal of a Foreign Correspondent, 1934–1941*. New York: Knopf, 1941, pp. 16–18.

2. Ian Kernshaw, *Hitler, 1936–1945: Nemesis*. New York: Norton, 2000, p. 841.

3. Robert G.L. Waite, *The Psychopathic God: Adolf Hitler*. New York: Da Capo Press, 1993, p. xi.

4. Quoted in Harold C. Deutsch, *The Conspiracy Against Hitler in the Twilight War*. Minneapolis: University of Minnesota Press, 1970, p. 32.

Chapter One: 1889–1919: The Wellsprings of Hate

5. Waite, *Psychopathic God*, p. 3.

6. Quoted in Waite, *Psychopathic God*, p. 56.

7. Quoted in John Toland, *Adolf Hitler*. Garden City, NY: Doubleday, 1976, p. 7.

8. Quoted in G.M. Gilbert, *The Psychology of Dictatorship*. New York: Ronald Press, 1950, p. 18.

9. Quoted in Toland, *Adolf Hitler*, p. 27.

10. Quoted in Joachim Fest, *Hitler*. New York: Harcourt Brace Jovanovich, 1974, pp. 30–31.

11. Adolf Hitler, *Mein Kampf (1925–26)*, trans. Ralph Manheim. Boston: Houghton Mifflin, 1971, p. 3.

12. Quoted in Waite, *Psychopathic God*, p. 109.

13. Quoted in William L. Shirer, *The Rise and Fall of the Third Reich: A History of Nazi Germany*. Greenwich, CT: Fawcett, 1960, p. 29.

14. Albert Speer, *Inside the Third Reich*. New York: Macmillan, 1970, p. 148.

15. Quoted in Waite, *Psychopathic God*, p. 11.

16. August Kubizek, *The Young Hitler I Knew*. trans. E.V. Anderson. Boston: Houghton Mifflin, 1955, p. 35.

17. Quoted in Waite, *Psychopathic God*, p. 19.

18. Quoted in Jeremy Noakes and Geoffrey Pridham, eds., *Documents on Nazism, 1919–1945*. New York: Viking Press, 1975, pp. 36–37.

19. Quoted in Shirer, *Rise and Fall of the Third Reich*, p. 54.

20. Crane Brinton et al., *A History of Civilization, 1815 to the Present*. Englewood Cliffs, NJ: Prentice-Hall, 1976, p. 759.

21. Erich Kahler, *The Germans*. Princeton: Princeton University Press, 1974, p. 280.

Chapter Two: 1919–1923: Rise of a Demagogue

22. Quoted in Henry C. Meyer, ed., *The Long Generation: Germany from Empire to Ruin, 1913–1945*. New York: Walker, 1973, p. 105.

23. Kernshaw, *Hitler*, p. xli.

24. Hitler, *Mein Kampf*, pp. 223–24.

25. Hitler, *Mein Kampf*, p. 354.

26. Hitler, *Mein Kampf*, p. 355.

27. Hitler, *Mein Kampf*, pp. 496–97.

28. Kahler, *Germans*, pp. 277–78.

29. Ernst Hanfstaengl, *The Missing Years*. London: Eyre and Spottiswoode, 1957, pp. 68–69.

30. Hanfstaengl, *Missing Years*, pp. 267–68.

31. Hitler, *Mein Kampf*, p. 56.

32. Quoted in Abraham Resnick, *The Holocaust*. San Diego: Lucent Books, 1991, p. 18.

33. Quoted in Norman H. Baynes, ed., *The Speeches of Adolph Hitler, April 1922–August 1939*. 2 vols. New York: Howard Fertig, 1969, vol. 1, pp. 86–87.

Chapter Three: 1923–1933: Triumph of the Will

34. Quoted in Waite, *Psychopathic God*, p. 75.

35. Kernshaw, *Hitler*, p. xliii.

36. Hitler, *Mein Kampf*, p. 672.

37. Hitler, *Mein Kampf*, p. 296.

38. Hitler, *Mein Kampf*, pp. 138–40.

39. Hitler, *Mein Kampf*, pp. 134–35, 289.

40. Quoted in Toland, *Adolf Hitler*, p. 227.

41. Speer, *Inside the Third Reich*, pp. 15–16.

42. Quoted in Baynes, *Speeches of Adolph Hitler*, vol. 1, p. 427.

Chapter Four: 1933–1939: A Nation Transformed

43. Waite, *Psychopathic God*, p. 75.

44. Quoted in Shirer, *Rise and Fall of the Third Reich*, p. 374.

45. Quoted in Shirer, *Rise and Fall of the Third Reich*, p. 376.

46. Quoted in Jeremy Noakes and Geoffrey Pridham, eds., *Nazism, 1919–1945, Vol. 1: The Rise to Power, 1919–1934, A Documentary Reader*. Exeter, UK: University of Exeter, 1983, p. 180.

47. Quoted in Kernshaw, *Hitler*, pp. 253–54.

48. Waite, *Psychopathic God*, p. 338.

49. Quoted in Baynes, *Speeches of Adolph Hitler*, vol. 1, p. 734.

50. Quoted in Waite, *Psychopathic God*, p. 41.

51. Winston S. Churchill, *The Gathering Storm*. Boston: Houghton Mifflin, 1948, pp. 189–90.

52. Louis L. Snyder, *The War: A Concise History, 1939–1945*. New York: Dell, 1960, p. 91.

53. Quoted in Snyder, *The War*, p. 82.

54. Quoted in Waite, *Psychopathic God*, p. 20.

Chapter Five: 1939–1942: The Third Reich at Its Zenith

55. Snyder, *The War,* pp. 296–97.

56. Quoted in Snyder, *The War,* pp. 82–83.

57. Quoted in Snyder, *The War,* p. 97.

58. Shirer, *Berlin Diary,* p. 421.

59. Quoted in Kernshaw, *Hitler,* p. 299.

60. Quoted in Snyder, *The War,* p. 154.

61. Quoted in Office of the United States Chief of Counsel for Prosecution of Axis Criminality, ed., *Nazi Conspiracy and Aggression.* 10 vols. Washington, DC: U.S. Government Printing Office, 1946, vol. 6, pp. 905–906.

62. Quoted in *Nazi Conspiracy and Aggression,* vol. 6, p. 931.

63. Quoted in *Nazi Conspiracy and Aggression,* vol. 4, p. 559.

64. Quoted in *Nazi Conspiracy and Aggression,* vol. 3, pp. 798–99.

65. Adolf Hitler, *Hitler's Secret Conversations.* New York: Signet, 1961, p. 501.

66. Quoted in Shirer, *Rise and Fall of the Third Reich,* p. 1256.

67. Shirer, *Rise and Fall of the Third Reich,* p. 1256.

68. Quoted in *Nazi Conspiracy and Aggression,* vol. 4, p. 563.

69. Quoted in *Nazi Conspiracy and Aggression,* vol. 4, pp. 787–90.

70. Quoted in Waite, *Psychopathic God,* p. 371.

Chapter Six: 1943–1945: Death of a Twisted Dream

71. Speer, *Inside the Third Reich,* p. 274.

72. Waite, *Psychopathic God,* pp. 372–73.

73. Winston S. Churchill, *The Second World War.* 6 vols. New York: Bantam, 1962, vol. 3, p. 511.

74. Quoted in Shirer, *Rise and Fall of The Third Reich,* p. 1310.

75. Snyder, *The War,* p. 463.

76. Quoted in Toland, *Adolf Hitler,* p. 811.

77. Quoted in Milton Shulman, *Defeat in the West.* Philadelphia: Trans-Atlantic Publications, 1995, p. 206.

78. Quoted in Felix Gilbert, *Hitler Directs His War.* New York: Oxford University Press, 1950, p. 106.

79. Heinz Guderian, *Panzer Leader.* New York: Ballantine, 1952, p. 341.

80. Quoted in Snyder, *The War,* p. 535.

81. Quoted in Kernshaw, *Hitler,* p. 832.

Epilogue: Monument to a Monster

82. Toland, *Adolph Hitler,* p. xiii.

83. Kernshaw, *Hitler,* p. 841.

84. Quoted in Victor Gollancz, *In Darkest Germany.* London: Victor Gollancz Ltd., 1947, p. 28.

85. Eberhard Jäckel, *Hitler in History.* Hanover, NH: Brandeis University Press, 1984, p. 106.

FOR FURTHER READING

Linda J. Altman, *The Holocaust, Hitler, and Nazi Germany.* Berkeley Heights, NJ: Enslow, 1999. A short but thoughtful introduction to Hitler and his crimes, aimed at junior high school readers.

Eleanor H. Ayer, *Adolph Hitler.* San Diego: Lucent Books, 1995. A general overview of Hitler's life and deeds, including his prosecution of the war in Europe against the Allies.

Cherese Cartlidge et al., *Life of a Nazi Soldier.* San Diego: Lucent Books, 2001. This well-written, informative volume explores the ranks of the German army during World War II, including data about command structure, weapons, methods of fighting, and the twisted Nazi ideology with which the soldiers were brainwashed. Highly recommended.

Eleanor R. Garner, *Eleanor's Story: An American Girl in Hitler's Germany.* Atlanta: PeachTree, 1999. Garner, whose parents moved with her to Germany just prior to the outbreak of World War II, presents her impressions of life in Hitler's police state. A powerful little book.

Eileen Hayes, *Children of the Swastika: The Hitler Youth.* Brookfield, CT: Millbrook Press, 1993. A disturbing exploration of the manner in which Hitler and his Nazi cronies effectively molded and twisted the minds of young Germans.

Don Nardo, *Franklin D. Roosevelt: U.S. President.* New York: Chelsea House, 1996. Hitler's American counterpart during World War II, Franklin Roosevelt, was in many ways the opposite of the German dictator—in intellect, personal character, worldview, and so on. This volume, aimed at young readers, effectively summarizes Roosevelt's contributions to the world, including his opposition to Nazi Germany.

Major Works Consulted

Norman H. Baynes, ed., *The Speeches of Adolf Hitler, April 1922–August 1939.* 2 vols. New York: Howard Fertig, 1969. An indispensable reference to Hitler's own words and ideas.

Eugene Davidson, *The Making of Adolf Hitler: The Birth and Rise of Nazism.* Columbia: University of Missouri Press, 1997. An excellent, well-documented overview of Hitler's rise to power.

E.J. Feuchtwanger, *From Weimar to Hitler: Germany, 1918–33.* New York: St. Martin's Press, 1993. This thoughtful volume explores the political, social, economic, and ideological conditions in Germany during the period when the Nazi Party rose to dominance.

Richard Grunberger, *The 12-Year Reich: A Social History of Nazi Germany, 1933–1945.* New York: Holt, Rinehart, and Winston, 1971. A large, highly informative look at German society during the years in which Hitler ruled it.

Alfons Heck, *The Burden of Hitler's Legacy.* Frederick, CO: Renaissance House, 1988. In this absorbing account, a German discusses how he, like many other German young people, became swept up in Nazism, only to witness it drag Germany to ruin. Heck explains how he came to see the truth and how he and the German people attempted to come to grips with their support of Nazism and its dark legacy. Highly recommended.

Adolf Hitler, *Mein Kampf, 1925–26,* trans. Ralph Manheim. Boston: Houghton Mifflin, 1971. Now easily seen as the often incoherent ramblings of a twisted mind, this is the Nazi bible that laid out many of Hitler's beliefs and ambitions.

Eberhard Jäckel, *Hitler in History.* Hanover, NH: Brandeis University Press, 1984. A short but thoughtful synopsis of Hitler's adult years by a respected German historian.

Ian Kernshaw, *Hitler, 1936–1945: Nemesis.* New York: Norton, 2000. The latest of several massive studies of Hitler and Nazism, this is easily one of the best. In stunning detail and with impressive documentation, Kernshaw, of England's Sheffield University, follows the Nazi dictator from his triumph at the 1936 Summer Olympics, to his persecution of the Jews and battle for European dominance, to his ignominious death in an underground bunker in 1945. Highly recommended.

August Kubizek, *The Young Hitler I Knew*, trans. E.V. Anderson. Boston: Houghton Mifflin, 1955. A fascinating eyewitness account of the young Adolf Hitler.

Roger Manvell, *Films and the Second World War*. New York: Dell, 1974. A very informative and readable synopsis of American, British, German, Japanese, and other films made for both propaganda and entertainment purposes during the war.

Otis C. Mitchell, *Hitler over Germany: The Establishment of the Nazi Dictatorship (1918–1954)*. Philadelphia: Institute for the Study of Human Issues, 1983. Well organized and fact-filled, this volume summarizes Hitler's political activities during his rise to power.

Office of the United States Chief of Counsel for Prosecution of Axis Criminality, ed., *Nazi Conspiracy and Aggression*. 10 vols. Washington, DC: U.S. Government Printing Office, 1946. For the historian or serious student of World War II, an extremely valuable collection of original documents pertaining to the Nazis.

Abraham Resnick, *The Holocaust*. San Diego: Lucent Books, 1991. A brief but solid introduction to Hitler's greatest single crime—the destruction of more than 6 million Jews.

Arnold P. Rubin, *The Evil That Men Do: The Story of the Nazis*. New York: Bantam, 1979. An effective overview of Hitler, his deadly regime, the Holocaust, and more.

William L. Shirer, *The Rise and Fall of the Third Reich: A History of Nazi Germany*. Greenwich, CT: Fawcett, 1960. One of the most important books ever produced about Hitler and his Reich, written by a noted American journalist and packed with eyewitness accounts and factual information. Highly recommended, though only serious students of the subject will want to wade through its more than 1,400 pages.

Louis L. Snyder, *The War: A Concise History, 1939–1945*. New York: Dell, 1960. A fast-paced, well-informed general overview of World War II that also contains a huge collection of excerpts from primary documents collected from numerous American and German sources, a number of which have been quoted.

Albert Speer, *Inside the Third Reich*. New York: Macmillan, 1970. The revealing memoir of one of Hitler's closest associates, chief Nazi architect and city planner Albert Speer. Highly recommended for serious students of Hitler and Nazism.

Jackson J. Spielvogel, *Hitler and Nazi Germany: A History*. Englewood Cliffs, NJ: Prentice-Hall, 1996. This recent volume is one of the two or three best overviews of Hitler's regime for general, nonscholarly readers.

John Toland, *Adolf Hitler*. Garden City, NY: Doubleday, 1976. One of the most massive and voluminously documented histories of Hitler and the Third Reich, with detailed information about Hitler's childhood and rise, conditions in Germany before and during World War II, Hitler's conduct of the war, the Holocaust, Germany's defeat by the Allies, and much more. Highly recommended for serious students.

Robert G.L. Waite, *The Psychopathic God: Adolf Hitler*. New York: Da Capo Press, 1993. An information-packed, meticulously documented, and thoroughly fascinating study of Hitler the man, including numerous speculative insights into his psychological makeup. Very highly recommended.

David Welch, *The Third Reich: Politics and Propaganda*. London: Routledge, 1993. An effective recent study of the way Hitler utilized propaganda to further his aims.

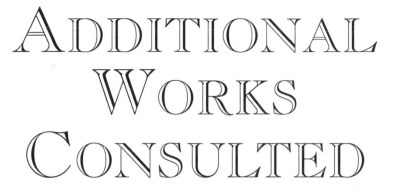

ADDITIONAL WORKS CONSULTED

William S. Allen, *The Nazi Seizure of Power: The Experience of a Single German Town, 1930–1935*. Chicago: Quadrangle Books, 1965.

Mark Arnold-Forster, *The World at War*. New York: Stein and Day, 1973.

Yahuda Bauer, *History of the Holocaust*. New York: Franklin Watts, 1982.

Edward W. Bennet, *German Rearmament and the West*. Princeton: Princeton University Press, 1979.

Richard Bessel, ed., *Life in the Third Reich*. New York: Oxford University Press, 1987.

C.E. Black and E.C. Helmreich, *Twentieth Century Europe: A History*. New York: Knopf, 1952.

Crane Brinton et al., *A History of Civilization, 1815 to the Present*. Englewood Cliffs, NJ: Prentice-Hall, 1976.

Martin Broszat, *Hitler and the Collapse of Weimar Germany*. New York: Berg, 1984.

F. L. Carsten, *The Rise of Fascism*. Berkeley: University of California Press, 1967.

Robert Cecil, *The Myth of the Master Race: Alfred Rosenberg and Nazi Ideology*. London: B.T. Batsford, 1972.

Winston S. Churchill, *The Gathering Storm*. Boston: Houghton Mifflin, 1948.

——, *The Second World War*. 6 vols. New York: Bantam, 1962.

——, *The War Speeches*, cd., Charles Eade. 3 vols. Boston: Houghton Mifflin, 1953.

Eugene Davidson, *The Unmaking of Adolf Hitler*. Columbia: University of Missouri Press, 1996.

Harold C. Deutsch, *The Conspiracy Against Hitler in the Twilight War*. Minneapolis: University of Minnesota Press, 1970.

Marshall Dill Jr., *Germany: A Modern History*. Ann Arbor: University of Michigan Press, 1961.

Joachim Fest, *Hitler*. New York: Harcourt Brace Jovanovich, 1974.

Klaus P. Fischer, *The History of Obsession: German Judeophobia and the*

Holocaust. New York: Continuum, 2001.

Michael Freeman, *Atlas of Nazi Germany*. New York: Macmillan, 1987.

Saul Friedlander, *Nazi Germany and the Jews: The Years of Persecution, 1933–1939*, Vol. 1. New York: HarperCollins, 1997.

Felix Gilbert, *Hitler Directs His War*. New York: Oxford University Press, 1950.

G.M. Gilbert, *The Psychology of Dictatorship*. New York: Ronald Press, 1950.

Victor Gollancz, *In Darkest Germany*. London: Victor Gollancz Ltd., 1947.

Heinz Guderian, *Panzer Leader*. New York: Ballantine, 1952.

Alan Guttmann, *The Olympics: A History of the Modern Games*. Chicago: University of Illinois Press, 1992.

Ernst Hanfstaengl, *The Missing Years*. London: Eyre and Spottiswoode, 1957.

Robert E. Herzstein, *Adolph Hitler and the German Trauma, 1913–1945: An Interpretation of the Nazi Phenomenon*. New York: G.P. Putnam's Sons, 1974.

John Hiden, *Germany and Europe, 1919–1939*. London: Longman Group, 1978.

Adolf Hitler, *Hitler's Secret Conversations*. New York: Signet, 1961.

———, *The Testament of Adolf Hitler*. London: Cassell, 1961.

William A. Jenks, *Vienna and the Young Hitler*. New York: Columbia University Press, 1960.

Gerrit P. Judd, *A History of Civilization*. New York: Macmillan, 1966.

Erich Kahler, *The Germans*. Princeton: Princeton University Press, 1974.

Walter C. Langer, ed., *Hitler Source Book* (from documents collected by the Office of Strategic Service, or OSS). National Archive, Washington, DC, 1946.

Leading Members of Nazi Party and German State, *Germany Speaks*. London: Thornton Butterworth, 1938.

Francis L. Loewenheim, ed., *Peace or Appeasement? Hitler, Chamberlain, and the Munich Crisis*. Boston: Houghton Mifflin, 1965.

Roger Manvell, *SS and Gestapo: Rule by Terror*. New York: Ballantine, 1969.

Henry C. Meyer, ed., *The Long Generation: Germany from Empire to Ruin, 1913–1945*. New York: Walker, 1973.

Hans Mommsen, *The Rise and Fall of Weimar Democracy*. Chapel Hill: University of North Carolina Press, 1996.

George L. Mosse, *Nazi Culture: Intellectual, Cultural, and Social Life in the Third Reich*. New York: Grosset and Dunlap, 1966.

Jeremy Noakes and Geoffrey Pridham, eds., *Documents on Nazism, 1919–1945*. New York: Viking Press, 1975.

———, *Nazism, 1919–1945, Vol. 1: The Rise to Power, 1919–1934, A*

Documentary Reader. Exeter, Eng.: University of Exeter, 1983.

————, *Nazism, 1919–1945, Vol. 2: State, Economy and Society, 1933-1939, A Documentary Reader.* Exeter, UK: University of Exeter, 1984.

Alison Owings, ed., *Frauen: German Women Recall the Third Reich.* New Brunswick, NJ: Rutgers University Press, 1993.

Detlev J.K. Peukert, *Inside Nazi Germany: Conformity, Opposition, and Racism in Everyday Life.* New Haven: Yale University Press, 1987.

Koppel S. Pinson, *Modern Germany: Its History and Civilization.* New York: Macmillan, 1966.

Abraham Resnick, *The Holocaust.* San Diego: Lucent Books, 1991.

A.J. Ryder, *Twentieth-Century Germany: From Bismark to Brandt.* New York: Columbia University Press, 1973.

William L. Shirer, *Berlin Diary: The Journal of a Foreign Correspondent, 1934–1941.* New York: Knopf, 1941.

Milton Shulman, *Defeat in the West.* Philadelphia: Trans-Atlantic Publications, 1995.

John L. Snell, *The Outbreak of the Second World War: Design or Blunder?* Boston: D.C. Heath, 1962.

Jonathan Steinberg, *All or Nothing: The Axis and the Holocaust, 1941–1943.* London: Routledge, 1994.

Simon Taylor, *The Rise of Hitler: Revolution and Counter-revolution in Germany, 1918–1933.* New York: Universe Books, 1983.

Robert-Hermann Tenbrock, *A History of Germany.* London: Longmans, Green, 1968.

Hannah Vogt, *The Burden of Guilt: A Short History of Germany, 1914–1945.* New York: Oxford University Press, 1964.

Gerhard L. Weinberg, *Germany, Hitler, and World War II: Essays in Modern Germany and World History.* New York: Cambridge University Press, 1995.

Chester Wilmot, *The Struggle for Europe.* Chicago: NTC Contemporary Publishing, 1998.

INDEX

Allies, 26, 66, 68, 78, 81–84, 89, 93
Anschluss, 59
Arts Academy, 17
Aryans, 16, 38–39, 61
astrology, 85
Auschwitz, 75–77
Austria, 15–17, 59–62

Babi Yar, 75
Beer Hall Putsch, 34–35
Belgium, 68
Belzec, 76
Berlin, 87, 90–91, 93
Berlin-Rome Axis, 60, 62
Berlin Wall, 93
Best, Werner, 53
Bismarck, Otto von, 46
Bloch, Edward, 14, 20
Blondi (Hitler's dog), 90
Braun, Eva (Hitler's mistress), 90
Braunau am Inn, 14, 16
Brinton, Crane, 22
Britain, 66–67, 70
   Battle of, 70, 82
Brownshirts. *See* SA
Buffum, David, 58
Bulge, Battle of the, 87
Burger, Adolf, 88

Chamberlain, Neville, 67
Churchill, Winston, 60–62, 69, 70, 81

concentration camps, 53
Czechoslovakia, 62

Dachau, 53
D day, 83–84
death, 18
Denmark, 68
Documents on Nazism (Noakes and
   Pridham), 28
Dresden, 82
Drexler, Anton, 32
Dunkerque, 69–70

East Germany, 93
Eiffel Tower, 66
Einsatzgruppen, 75
Einstein, Albert, 55
Enabling Act, 45–46
England. *See* Britain
English Channel, 70

Federal Republic of Germany, 93
Films and the Second World War
   (Manville), 48
Final Solution, 74–75
First Reich, 46
France, 66–70, 83–84

German Democratic Republic, 93
German Workers' Party, 27
Germany

attacks Poland, 62
captured by Russians, 87
cities raided in, 82
declares war on Allies, 66
early history of, 15–16
economic problems of, 26–27, 42–43
Great Britain and France declare war on, 66–67
loses World War I, 21–23
reunification of, 59–62
surrenders to Allies, 92–93
Gestapo, 52–55, 66
Goebbels, Joseph, 40, 57, 69–70, 82, 85
Goering, Hermann. *See* Göring, Hermann
Göring, Hermann, 21, 40
Graf, Joseph, 61
Great Britain. *See* Britain
Great Depression, 42
Guderian, Heinz, 87

Hamburg, 82
Hanfstaengl, Erna, 28
Hanfstaengl, Ernst, 31
Heredity and Racial Biology for Students (Graf), 61
Herr Wolf. *See* Hitler, Adolf
Hiedler, Johann. *See* Hitler, Johann
Himmler, Heinrich, 40, 52–53, 73–74, 89
Hindenburg, Paul von, 45, 52
Hitler, Adolf
autobiographical films about, 48, 49
birth of, 14
career of

banned from speaking in public, 40–41
becomes propaganda officer, 27–29
as chancellor, 45, 50–52
failed coup attempt by, 34–35
foreign policies adopted by, 59–62
founds SA, 28–29
joins German Workers' Party, 27
money printing scheme of, 88
officers plot killing of, 84–87
orders the killing of Jews, 73–77
as painter, 17, 20
writes *Mein Kampf*, 36
childhood of, 14–15
commits suicide, 90
education of, 16–17
enlists in German army, 20–21
hatred of Jews by, 18–21, 37, 39
personality of, 10–11, 13–14
attempts to impress women by, 21
becomes fascinated with Germany's past, 15–16
fascination with wolves, 19
hatred of the Jews by, 18–21, 37, 39
infatuated with death, 18
public speaking techniques of, 26–27, 29–32
temper of, 17–18, 65, 87–89
physical characteristics of, 12–13
Hitler, Alois, Jr. (Adolf's half-brother), 14
Hitler, Johann (Adolf's grandfather), 14

Hitler, Klara (Adolf's mother), 14, 20
Hitler Youth movement, 56
Holland, 68
Holocaust, 73–77, 93
Holy Roman Empire, 15, 46
Höss, Rudolf, 75
House of Habsburg, 15

Italy, 66, 83

Jäckel, Eberhard, 52, 93
Japan, 66
Jews
    arrests of, 53
    Graf lists "inferior traits" of, 61
    Hilter's extermination of, 73–77,
        79–81, 91
    Hitler's hatred of, 18–21, 37, 39
    Nazis loot homes of, 57–59
    Wagner's views about, 16

Kahler, Erich, 23, 29
Kernshaw, Ian, 9, 25, 38, 93
Koch, Erich, 73
Kohler, Pauline, 21
Kristallnacht. See Night of the Broken
    Glass
Kubizek, August, 13, 18

Lake Toplitz, 88
Lebensraum, 39, 62
Leningrad, 82
London, 70
Luftwaffe, 65, 70
Luxembourg, 68

Manville, Roger, 48
May, Karl, 28
Mein Kampf (Adolf Hitler), 36–38, 57,
    71
Modern Germany (Pinson), 26
Moscow, 82
Mousse, George, 61
Muller, Karl von, 28
Munich, 20, 27
Munich Observer (newspaper), 28
Mussolini, Benito, 60, 66, 83

National Socialist German Workers'
    Party (NSDAP), 27–29, 34
National Socialists. See Nazis
Nazi Culture (Mousse), 61
Nazis
    gain electoral power, 45
    increase in membership of, 28
    portrayal of, in movies, television,
        and books, 11
    treatment of Jews by, 57–59
Nazism, 1919–1945 (Noakes and
    Pridham), 58
Night of the Broken Glass, 57–59
Night of the Long Knives, 53–54
Noakes, Jeremy, 28, 58
Normandy, 83
Norway, 68
NSDAP. See National Socialist German
    Workers' Party
Nuremberg, 8, 48, 93

Operation Barbarossa, 71
Operation Sea Lion, 70

Papen, Franz von, 45
Paris, 68, 87
Pinson, Koppel S., 26
Poland, 62, 64, 66
Pridham, Geoffrey, 28, 58
Psychopathic God, The (Waite), 19, 65

RAF. *See* Royal Air Force
Reck-Malleczewen, Fredrich, 32, 34
Reich Chamber of Culture, 57
Reichstag, 45, 52, 73
Riefenstahl, Leni, 48–49
Rise and Fall of the Third Reich (Shirer), 71
Rise of Hitler (Taylor), 32
Röhm, Ernst, 29, 34, 52–55
Romania, 70, 87
Rome, 83
Royal Air Force (RAF), 70
Rundstedt, Marshal Gerd von, 87
Russia, 70–73, 81–82

SA
    eliminated by Hitler, 53–54
    failed coup attempt by, 34–35
    formation of, 28–29
Saint Petersburg, 72
Schachleiter, Abbot Alban, 28
Schutzstaffel. See SS
Second Reich, 46
Shicklgruber, Alois (Adolf's father), 14
Shirer, William L., 8, 68, 71, 73
Sicily, 83
60 Minutes II (news program), 88

Slavs, 72–73
Snyder, Louis, 62, 64, 84
Speer, Albert, 17, 43, 78–79, 93
SS, 52–55, 66, 72–73, 75
Stalin, Joseph, 62, 70
Stalingrad, 82
Stauffenberg, Claus S. von, 84–86
Streicher, Julius, 40
Struggle for Europe (Wilmot), 85
Sturmabteilung. See SA
swastika, 29, 66

Taylor, Simon, 32
Third Reich, 45–46, 64, 77
Toland, John, 91
Treaty of Versailles, 21, 59–60
Treblinka, 76–77
Tripartite Pact, 66
Triumph of the Will (Riefenstahl), 48–49

U-boats, 78

Vienna, 17

Wagner, Richard, 16, 19
Waite, Robert G.L.
    on the extent of Hitler's power, 12
    on Hitler's fascination with wolves, 19
    on Hitler's opponents misunderstanding him, 50
    on Hitler's personality, 10, 65
    on military consequences of Hitler exterminating Jews, 69–81

on why Germans were drawn to Hitler, 56–57

War Speeches of Churchill, The (Churchill), 69

Wehrmacht, 64

Weimar Republic. *See* Germany

Weltanschauung, 40

Werwolf (Hitler's headquarters), 19

West Germany, 93

William (Wilhelm) II, 26

Wilmot, Chester, 85

Wolfsschanze (Hitler's headquarters), 19

Wolfsschlucht (Hitler's headquarters), 19

wolves, 19

Wolzek, 77

World War I, 20–23

Young Hitler I Knew, The (Kubizek), 13

Zyklon B, 77

PICTURE CREDITS

ABOUT THE AUTHOR

Historian and award-winning author Don Nardo has written several books for young adults about modern military conflicts and their leaders, including *The Mexican–American War*, *World War II in the Pacific*, *Franklin D. Roosevelt: U.S. President*, and *The War Against Iraq*. He has also published a two-volume history of Japan, the nation that collaborated with Hitler's Germany against the Allies. Mr. Nardo lives with his wife, Christine, in Massachusetts.